KIMBERLEY SELDON'S
Business of Design™
Part 1

What they don't teach you in design school!

WRITTEN BY: **KIMBERLEY SELDON**

Kimberley Seldon Design Group
Kimberley Seldon Productions, Inc.
909 Mount Pleasant Road
Toronto, Ontario M4P 2Z6
www.kimberleyseldon.com

ISBN: 1450553850
ISBN-13: 9781450553858

ACKNOWLEDGEMENTS
Editing: Alex Newman and Brian Koturbash
Marketing: Cheryl Horne
Support: Cheryl Horne, Linda Jennings, Aysun Kuck, Erin Mercer, Kathy Seale, Bret Tinson
Additional Support: Michael Tafts, owner of G. Pederson and Associates Construction
Cover Photography: Tim Leyes
Cover Sketch: Erin Mercer
Interior Illustrations: Tania LaCaria

Limit of Liability/Disclaimer of Warranty:

What they're saying about
Kimberley Seldon's Business of Design™

Thank you to the thousands of talented design professionals who have taken my courses, **Kimberley Seldon's Business of Design™: Parts** 1 – 2. By candidly sharing your experience, strength and hope in class you have helped write this series of books. Your generosity of spirit is unmatched and I think of you all as I strive to improve my practices. May you be happy and successful in business and in life.

Comments from past **Kimberley Seldon's Business of Design™** seminar attendees:

"As a newbie in the industry, I was frustrated with 'closed lips'. Finally, someone with the courage to tell all!" – Tamara, Edmonton

"Kimberley simplified large intentions into real, doable, manageable steps." – Joanne, Toronto

"Process Management and Strategy has been the most difficult for me to buy into until Kimberley presented a solution." – Joy, Toronto

"A heartfelt thank you. It is so clear why you are such a success in life and in business. You are a tremendous inspiration to me and many." – Alli, Toronto

"I had considered retirement, but now I will just change my strategy!" – J.B., Calgary

"This information is not covered in traditional design school and yet is absolutely critical to success in the design industry." – Lisa, Calgary

"I enjoyed the weekend. I came away with so many valuable ideas. I just can't thank you enough. It was stellar!" – Sarah, Vancouver

"I gave myself a raise and doubled my income this past year thanks to Kimberley's guidance!" – Monica, Dallas

"I really appreciated Kimberley's honest approach to topics, rarely are professionals honest about mistakes or problems!" – Heather, Burlington

"Kimberley is fantastic! Her energy and enthusiasm is infectious." – Kelly, Los Angeles

"Kimberley provides practical advice and clearly demonstrates her integrity and honesty!" – Norah, Toronto

Contents at a Glance

Although ambitious, my goal is to condense nearly 20 years of learning into these workbooks (**Kimberley Seldon's Business of Design™: Part 1 and Part 2**). The lessons I pass on were generously shared with me and they will work for you too.

Here's what you can expect from Kimberley Seldon's Business of Design™: Part 1

- **Inspiration for moving forward**. A renewed commitment to yourself, your goals and <u>your life</u>. You don't need a design for working! You need a **Design for Living**.

- **Design for Living**. A blueprint for your career and life. A five year vision used as a daily gauge to measure every decision. Plus, guidance on building an **Action Plan** which allows you to realize your **Design for Living**.

- **Satisfaction by Design**. Incentive to work toward specific systems and procedures which are necessary to reach project goals with reliability and accuracy. Increased motivation and direction for evaluating how your business works.

- **Client Insight and Contentment**. The client is always right. Working in a systematic fashion allows you to consistently satisfy a majority of clients.

- **Resource Management**. A specific guide for building an "A" Team and working in harmony through agreed upon rules known as the **Resource Guide to Excellence (RGE)**.

- **Charging for your Expertise**. Determining your value as a design professional. Billing and collecting with ease. **Elimination of cash flow issues**.

Table of Contents

About the Author: Kimberley Seldon

I never intended to write a book about the business of design. I've been busy, running my own interior design firm and writing about interior design, decorating and architecture in magazines and newspapers for nearly 20 years. But the *business of design*? Who has time?

Like you, I'm so busy working, there's precious little time for pursuing other interests; even worthwhile interests like authorship. And yet, the idea of the **Kimberley Seldon's Business of Design**™ kept returning to me until I finally surrendered and put pen to paper.

I've been practicing interior design since graduating from design school in 1991. A native of Los Angeles, I moved to Toronto when I married and determined that the career I'd had up until that time (producing and writing for television) was too demanding for a woman starting a family. Little did I know I was trading one adrenaline-powered occupation for another!

For those of you who remember, 1991 was a tough year – there was a recession and jobs were scarce. Even offering my services for free, I found no prospects for employment. With two small children at home, I only wanted to work part time so it seemed the only obvious choice was to go into business for myself. How hard could it be? If you're reading this book, I assume you know exactly how hard it can be.

In 1996 I'd been "dabbling" in the profession for five years, taking on the occasional client and fitting the work around my life as a young mother. During this time I was asked to make a first television appearance on the lifestyle program **Real Life with Erica Ehm**. My job was to provide entertaining information about decorating.

I knew I found my true calling from that first appearance. In short time I was appearing on a variety of shows and fielding offers for a show of my own. It was a heady time and I found myself "cramming" to become the expert I portrayed on TV.

Simultaneously, I started working as a stylist for shelter magazines. The first assignment - to produce a Christmas story in the middle of July for **Style at Home** magazine – turned into a satisfying 12-year relationship (and counting) and I'm grateful to former Editor Gail

Johnston-Habs for offering me a position as contributing Decorating Editor (and to Karl Lohnes for making that introduction possible.)

Two years later, I got my dream job -- hosting and producing a one-hour special titled, "Shopping the Paris Flea Market" for **HGTV-USA**. I loved Paris – spending most of my vacation hours there exploring the Marche aux Puces. I was asked to craft a one-hour tour of the highlights, toss in a few French expressions (pas de problème) and make sure the viewers learned something along the way. The special was well-received and I quickly had several job offers.

I turned down most of them, though, because they called for me to wear overalls, wield a hammer or produce faux finishes; interesting tasks but none appropriate for a professional interior designer nor befitting the glamorous career I'd envisioned for myself. In contrast, the producers at **HGTV-Canada** approached me and asked only what kind of show I thought I might like to host. Without a moment's hesitation I replied, "I've never been to Italy." And that is precisely how **Design for Living with Kimberley Seldon** was born.

In its nearly 200 episodes, **Design for Living with Kimberley Seldon** travelled the world filming the best interiors for an audience thirsty for good design. As the host I interviewed interior designers, decorators and architects from North America, Europe, Asia and Africa, garnering for myself a priceless education from the most talented people in the profession.

I consider this period of my life to have been my true interior design education. However, none of it prepared me for the actual *business* of design. And that's where this story really begins…

Guide to Icons throughout the Book

 At a glance. Here's a summary of what's ahead in each chapter.

 Sharpen your pencil. These exercises are suggested - the same way donning a parachute before you jump from a plane is suggested.

 Red flags. Be very careful. These ideas/actions can trip you up.

 Resentment and a Coffee Maker. Popular, though not terribly compelling reasons for becoming and/or being the boss.

 Take it to the bank. Key phrases and remarks; worth reading twice.

Glossary of Terms

Action Plan   The creation of tasks and/or step-by-step guidance for the purpose of accomplishing goals on your **Design for Living**.

Cash Flow   Money coming into and going out of a company.

Deficiency   A deficiency (or punch list item) refers to a detail that requires repair or further attention at the summation of a project.

Design for Living   A personal vision statement designed to capture key desires and goals for your business and your life.

Income   Money a company receives by providing its services.

KSDG   Kimberley Seldon Design Group.

Markup   A fee (charged to a customer) over and above the cost of an item or service, that contributes to the company's income.

Mission Statement   A mission statement is a short written announcement detailing a company's purpose and projecting its vision; an overview of your company's core ideology.

Profit   Profit (also called net income or earnings) is the money a business has left after it pays its operating expenses, taxes, and other current bills.

RGE   **Resource Guide to Excellence** – rules of governance, which apply to trades who are working for you on behalf of clients.

Satisfaction by Design   Reliance on a systematic and structured set of procedures to complete projects on time, on budget, with consistently pleasing results.

Spark   An off-hand comment (occasionally sounds like a "joke") that seems easier to ignore than deal with directly.

Turnkey Service   A system where all furniture and furnishings ordered on behalf of a client are received and warehoused until every item to complete the project is "in hand", ready to be delivered and installed at the job site.

Foreword

Welcome to all of you – interior designers, decorators, stagers, stylists, landscapers, architects, organizers, decorative artists and other industry professionals who want to embark on building or re-designing your business practice. This text and workbook unveils insights I've cultivated during 20 years as a practicing interior design professional. It's also the culmination of many years of working steadily with a professional business coach, Marysia Czarski. Marysia's intelligence and impeccable standards have transformed my business and my life into something far more meaningful (and lucrative) over the years.

In addition to a passion for design and some raw talent, I've worked tirelessly to improve both my craft and business practices. Many of the lessons I share with you in this book were learned the proverbial "hard way." I guarantee the techniques and advice found within these pages can save you from making many of the same mistakes I made.

Kimberley Seldon's Business of Design™ is an instructive guide to creating a unique blueprint for running your own successful design practice. It's not *theory* -- there's plenty of that on the market already. Instead, it's specific and detailed – a concrete formula for success that took years for me to build, and one that works equally for the sole proprietor and the multi-employee operation.

Flip through any home design magazine and marvel at the beautiful rooms inside. These photos make our work look easy. In reality of course, it's anything but easy. We know how much blood, sweat and negotiation stands between the initial client meeting and the finished photography. The management of trades, staff and clients is a complex process and most of us have little or no training to prepare us for the intricacies a "typical" job provides.

Kimberley Seldon's Business of Design™ carefully reconstructs best business practices – from project initiation to completion, and every detail in between.

Kimberley Seldon's Business of Design™ provides both novice and seasoned professionals with the skills and confidence required to deliver every job on time, on budget, with consistently pleasing results, exactly as promised.

On a personal note, I also want to ignite a renewed enthusiasm for running your own rewarding design practice. This is a career that breeds isolation. I know this from personal experience and through teaching the live version of Kimberley Seldon's Business of Design™ to more than 2,000 participants. Many design professionals feel lost and alone, having no clear idea of where to turn when they need practical advice. Kimberley Seldon's Business of Design™ can help.

 Although for reasons of efficiency, I use the terms "design firm," "design professional" and "designer," I know many other professionals will benefit from this book. The fundamentals outlined here apply to anyone in the field of architecture, interior design, decorating, staging, styling, landscaping and other "creative" professions that work on an hourly fee.

Let's get started.

In **Chapter One** we consider the daily frustrations that leave you wondering why you didn't follow your mom's advice and take up accounting, or work for your father, or marry a doctor.

Designing the Future

In this Chapter

- Section 1: Why you Bought this Book
- Section 2: What this Book can do for You

Why did you buy this book? Don't get me wrong; I'm glad you did. But, there must be some reason (or many reasons?) you feel compelled to lay down hard earned dollars and purchase a book about running a design business. After all, you are already running a design business, right?

And if you are already running a design business I know you are busy; likely putting in way too many hours and finding it difficult to create balance. I know you feel isolated; wedged between clients and trades. I know you are frustrated and miserable when projects veer off course or don't turn out the way you want them to. I know you are willing to work longer hours, forgo exercise routines and limit family holidays just to keep projects on track. I know money is not your primary motivation; you really want to create something beautiful and lasting.

How do I know all this? Because I'm just like you; I have walked in your shoes. I'll bet you begin every project with the best intentions, vowing to do whatever it takes to make the client happy and avoid the mistakes of the past. Right? Of course you do, what design professional doesn't want this?

The problem is that project difficulties cannot be corrected or eliminated by applying the same methods that created the problems in the first place.

> **Insanity** = doing the same thing over and over again and expecting different results. *Albert Einstein*

If you're already in business for yourself, you've likely discovered it takes more than raw talent, hard work and perseverance to run a successful design practice.

Section 1: Why you Bought this Book

Why did you decide to buy this book? If you're like me, you think of yourself as a creative person, with a desire to produce something beautiful and meaningful. That's what attracted you to this business in the first place, isn't it? Perhaps your dream is to decorate beautiful homes or design country gardens or manage new home construction projects or develop high-rise condominiums. If you're already in business for yourself, you've likely discovered it takes more than raw talent, hard work and perseverance to run a successful design practice. (Don't worry; by the time you get to the end of the book, you'll know what it really *does* take to run a successful design practice.)

Here are some excellent reasons for purchasing this book:

1. You're already in business and you realize you don't know everything.

2. You'd like to start your own business but have never worked within a successful design firm environment before.

3. You want to make clients happy – or happy more frequently.

4. You want to develop lasting, rewarding relationships with trades and suppliers.

5. You long to have a team of employees (or at least an assistant) to share the load.

6. You want to earn more money. . . (or some money!)

7. You've made some mistakes – maybe some big mistakes!

8. You have natural talent; your friends think you should turn "professional".

9. You made promises you thought you could keep, but others let you down.

10. You haven't had a vacation since Clinton was in the White House.

I've given you a few reasons why you may have bought this book, but surely you have others. Think about the work you do daily and year after year. What types of problems, both general and specific do you encounter? Do you find yourself wishing you had a trusted peer who could advise you? What tasks leave you longing for an assistant? Perhaps what used to be an occasional desire to "leave it all behind" has become a near-constant refrain?

You are not alone. But before we can solve the issues, we have to name them.

EXERCISE #1: Why I Bought this Book

Write down your own reasons for buying this book – be as detailed as possible. Consider practices that are not working for you; problems that occur with regularity.

1. _____

_____

2. _____

_____

3. _____

_____

4. _____

_____

5. _____

_____

6. _____

_____

7. _____

_____

8. _____

_____

9. _____

_____

10. _____

_____

This exercise is available for download at www.businessofdesign.com/worksheets.

Section 2: What this Book can do for You

What would you like to gain from **Kimberley Seldon's Business of Design**™? For example, make more money, gain new clients, increase vacation time and satisfy clients on a consistent basis?

EXERCISE #2: What can this book do for you?

List your thoughts and needs here.

1. _____
2. _____
3. _____
4. _____
5. _____
6. _____
7. _____
8. _____
9. _____
10. _____
11. _____
12. _____
13. _____
14. _____
15. _____
16. _____

This exercise is available for download at www.businessofdesign.com/worksheets.
Kimberley Seldon's Business of Design™ can do all this and more. Keep reading.

It's a bumpy road to becoming "the boss" and enjoying corporate maturity. And most of us have the bruises to prove it!

In **Chapter Two** we'll review lessons from my very first client and answer the question, "Are we having fun yet?"

And, I'll tell you how a funny thing happened on the way to the cash register...

ARE WE HAVING FUN YET?!

The Birth of a Business
Resentment and a Coffee Maker

In this Chapter

- Section 1: Infancy
- Section 2: Toddlerhood
- Section 3: Are we having fun yet?

Most sole proprietors begin their careers by working for someone else. While employed, they dream of being the boss, fantasizing about how ideal things would be if only they were in charge. The employee imagines that clients would be happier, since they would never make the foolish mistakes that occur at the present place of employment and they could do the work faster, better and more stylishly. How did the boss get so many clients anyway -- and with so little talent and charm? Hmmmm.

The employee is certain the boss is making tons of money, but downplays this so as not to arouse jealousy in the all-deserving and underpaid who make up the payroll. The employee dreams of 4-week vacations, two or three times a year, paid for by the company and "written off". This is a mysterious concept, which somehow translates into free money. Being the owner means freedom. None of this accounting for one's time, allotting a miserly number of vacation days to the calendar, or answering to anyone else's imposed schedule. And all of this would be possible if only the hardworking, so-much-smarter-than-the-boss employee were running his/her own business.

Positive the boss is making tons of money, the employee reaches a point of no return. And when the boss has done something offensive or ridiculous, such as questioning the employee's absence or holding him/her accountable for a project error, the employee decides it's time to branch out on their own. I call this:

 Resentment and a Coffee Maker

With a little resentment and a good coffee maker the entrepreneur launches a design firm or other business and announces with all the arrogance endowed to the untested, "Looks like I'm the competition now." The former boss watches this with mild amusement and even affection. Life may not be quite as idyllic for the new shop owner as imagined, but hands are shaken and best wishes are sent as "the competition" is born.

What's next? Well, we all know that after birth… comes infancy.

Section 1: Infancy

What do we know of infants? We can all agree they are self centered, unregulated, and dependent on others for survival. Infants require constant supervision, untiring devotion and all-encompassing attention. They have no set patterns and no concept of day or night. Yes, they are sometimes adorable, but most agree caring for an infant is a lot of work!

> Design firms in their infancy are no different, except our growth is not a linear development phase. While a baby outgrows the infant stage relatively quickly, in business this period can go on indefinitely.

Indefinitely? Yes. Forever.

My life as an infant designer started with working for the friend of a friend. She had heard I was a design school graduate and had a lovely home. The client (let's call her Mrs. A) phoned me to ask for help with her decorating project. Because I didn't have a lot of experience in the profession of interior design I decided to give her a really good price for my services. In fact, this was a deal that no one would turn down. I told Mrs. A that I wouldn't charge her for any of my time. Instead, I would charge a 10% markup on any items she purchased. Who would refuse such a great deal?

Such a great deal.

You can imagine what happened. I would arrive at Mrs. A's house for a scheduled appointment to find her on the phone or busy with her baby. One time she asked me to hold her baby while she finished her pedicure. After 20 or 30 minutes delay, while I waited to get her attention, we might start discussing actual decorating needs. I patiently guided her through every aspect of the project -- providing floor plans, elevations, colour and furniture direction and a great deal of my time. Still, I was optimistic that my efforts would be rewarded when we finally started making purchases. (Are you cringing? Have you been here? Are you here now?)

We did do some shopping. We even made a few purchases. At one point, I was asked to source coffee tables and end tables. I visited every store in town and narrowed down suitable options for Mrs. A's approval. Since she was struggling to make a decision, I suggested she visit the stores with me. At the appointed hour I drove to Mrs. A's house and picked her up. We visited half a dozen stores and enjoyed our time together finding everything on our list. We determined to buy our choices on the following Monday but...

...a funny thing happened on the way to the cash register.

Over the weekend, my client's mother-in-law decided to get rid of all her furniture to redecorate, and offered it to my client. Fortunately for Mrs. A that meant she wouldn't have to buy anything new at all. "How lucky," I replied... and how foolish I felt. After all, our little shopping excursion had me laying out money for a babysitter for my children and gas for my car, not to mention sacrificing more of my time.

Are we having fun yet?

Perhaps I'm not a fast learner. I'm the type of person who thinks, "If I just do it better, if I get more organized, if I apply myself with more fervor... I can do this, I can do this, I can do this!" The first time the client had me cooling my heels for twenty minutes in her living room, a smart person would have said, "This isn't going to work. I can't make money like this."

Was my growing resentment Mrs. A's fault? Absolutely not. Who wouldn't want to inherit lovely furniture from a relative? I couldn't honestly blame her for my dissatisfaction with our working agreement. After all, I created it! Instead of reproaching Mrs. A for my wasted time, I have become eternally grateful for what she taught me.

Here's what my first client taught me:

- I am the one who determines my value and worth in a relationship.

- Clients respect my time and expertise when I do.

- The expertise I provide is valuable and worthy of compensation.

- It is within my power to change the rules of the game.

Sound familiar? Your details may be different but I'll bet most of you have done something equally naïve at the infancy stage of your career.

Maybe you are currently in the infancy stage, and perhaps you've been there for a very long time. Don't despair.

There is a solution.

EXERCISE #3: The Infancy Stage

List the ways you feel your business is in its infancy. Review the frustrations you experience as it relates to this stage of growth.

1. _____

2. _____

3. _____

4. _____

5. _____

6. _____

7. _____

8. _____

9. _____

10. _____

11. _____

12. _____

13. _____

14. _____

15. _____

This exercise is available for download at www.businessofdesign.com/worksheets.

This exercise is not meant to be discouraging. **Kimberley Seldon's Business of Design**™ can fast track you to a new level of maturity. But first, we need to determine gaps in knowledge and uncover those areas where growth is possible.

Section 2: Toddlerhood

I hate to be the bearer of bad news but if you had difficulties in the infancy stage, watch out! Parents who are reading this will agree that a toddler is considerably more demanding than an infant.

Full of questions and always on the go. A toddler is stubborn personified because this little person now thinks he/she knows a thing or two. Unreasonable, erratic and constantly in motion, a toddler is an insatiable and unstable beast.

Unfortunately many "creative" businesses end up in the toddler stage indefinitely. While a human lifespan allows for a mercifully short toddler period, in business this stage has no definitive ending. As we struggle to improve our expertise we vow, "I'm going to make this work. I will work harder. I will work faster. I will add staff. I'll be more organized. I'll get up early. I'll stay up late. I can do it, I can do it, I can do it". Tell me that doesn't sound like a toddler.

 No wonder so many business owners quit in frustration.

What? Quit? Not me. Sure, I'm Bitter, Angry, Disappointed and Resentful (like some twisted version of the Dwarfs), but you would be too if you had my clients/employees/trades/luck. However, I'm no quitter. I will keep pushing myself until I get it right. I'll work weekends and evenings. I won't take a vacation and I won't take a salary, not until my business really takes off. Besides, I love my work, really. I don't see it as a sacrifice. I'm happy to put in whatever hours it takes to build my business. Sound familiar?

The problem is… there's no finish line.

This vague goal of getting the business to "take off" is never fully defined and frankly, never seems in danger of being fulfilled. There's always some other project/task/client stopping you from working a civilized number of hours or taking a vacation or exercising or eating dinner with your family or enjoying a living wage or (go ahead, add your own):

If you're in the dreaded toddler stage, doing what you're doing now, making the money you're making today, working the hours you're working regularly, getting the meager satisfaction you get presently, taking the few vacation days you enjoy annually, is this enough? How many years do you want to continue doing this? This is the question I asked myself:

Is it time to want more?

 When I teach the live seminar of **Kimberley Seldon's Business of Design**™, I meet a lot of designers at the toddler stage. Some of them have been there for twenty or thirty years and they are exhausted. What's worse, they're also Bitter, Angry, Disappointed and Resentful.

My first client experience – with Mrs. A – left me feeling put upon, underappreciated, foolish and disrespected. Of course, I would never show these hurt feelings to the client. I pretended things were fine. I just kept smiling and taking it, taking it, taking it. But multiply that over ten clients, over ten years and you can see how easy it is for Bitter, Angry, Disappointed and Resentful to take up residence in your soul.

EXERCISE #4: The Toddler Stage

List the ways you feel your business is in its toddlerhood. Review the frustrations you experience as it relates to this stage of growth.

1. _____

2. _____

3. _____

4. _____

5. _____

6. _____

7. _____

8. _____

9. _____

10. _____

11. _____

12. _____

13. _____

14. _____

15. _____

This exercise is available for download at www.businessofdesign.com/worksheets.

What would you say if I told you it's likely the client isn't feeling any better than you are…

Section 3: Are we having fun yet?

Ever notice the nearly mass dissatisfaction with our industry? I have yet to be at a cocktail or dinner party, where somebody doesn't bring up some sort of horror story about renovating, interior design, decorating or landscaping. You go to a friend's house and remark on her beautiful new kitchen and the response is: "Really? You cannot believe what I went through with my contractor/architect/decorator/designer/feng shui expert (fill in the blank)." Why is that? (More about client relationships in **Chapter 6**)

If you're a sole proprietor working 24/7 with low income, no time off, frequently unhappy clients, why do you keep doing it? I found myself in just that position. Working so many hours I never went for lunch, exercised, or had my hair done. My clients looked great and I looked... tired! No one came to me and said, "Honey, you've got this all wrong."

If this is your life as 'the boss' you should work for somebody else. As an employee you work 9-5, take three weeks vacation and costly mistakes don't come out of your paycheck. Employees don't hire or fire staff or lay awake at night when cash flow dries up. What's not to like?

 Why did you want to be the boss anyway? Was it resentment and a pot of coffee that launched you as the owner of a design firm? Was it the promise of unlimited cash, rewarding work, glory, fame and abundant free time? As Dr. Phil would say, "How's that workin' for you?"

Shouldn't being a business owner enrich your life? Doesn't it seem reasonable that it should allow you to enjoy a lifestyle that is abundant in every way including health, wealth, leisure and success?

If you're like I was, you may tell people that you love the freedom of being a business owner, but are you really free? Or, are you acting like I was, as if my life's mission was to work - 24/7? If so, you've been operating with a design for working – what I'm about to show you is a **Design for Living** (explained in **Chapter 3**).

In the next chapter, we begin to build that foundation by completing a personal **Design for Living** and an **Action Plan** designed to help you realize your goals. This is where you move beyond **Infancy** and **Toddlerhood**... and plant the seeds to grow a **Mature Business**. Does that sound good? You bet it does.

****

Complete **Exercises** 1 - 4 before moving on to the next section.

****

Mature businesses start with a solid foundation; a vision of where the owner wants to be in the next Five-Ten-Fifteen-Twenty years and beyond. In **Chapter Three** we begin to build that vision.

Plus, the sign you've been waiting for.

And, I'll tell you how I crossed paths with Oprah, Tyra and Ellen.

CHAPTER THREE
A Design for Living

In this Chapter

- Section 1: Create a Personal Design for Living
- Section 2: The Power of a Personal Design for Living
- Section 3: Putting your Design for Living into Action
- Section 4: Building the Foundation for a Mature Business

If you could design the perfect life, what would it look like? Let's say it's five years in the future. Are you making money? Traveling? Do you have a lot of clients or only one client who's fabulously wealthy?

Are you on television? Have you written a book? Do you have a blog or newsletter? Is your name on the front door of a retail store or a line of furniture? What's your reputation, are you known locally, nationally or internationally?

Do you work from home or have an office with 10 staff? Are you part of a collective of like minded individuals who rent downtown space?

Do you have a family? Do you spend flexible time with your family and friends? How much? When do you exercise? When was the last time you had a vacation where you didn't take work along?

I asked myself those exact questions years ago. And you know what? I did not like my answers.

Someone asked me once to imagine my funeral and hear what the attendees had to say about me. I heard all right. They said:

"Poor dear. She worked herself to death."

Section 1: Create your own Design for Living

What does your ideal life look like five years from now?

EXERCISE #5: Design for Living

In the space below, describe in detail where you see yourself in five years. Think big; don't worry about how you will make any of it happen, just list in vivid detail what you'd like your life to look like in five years. Be specific and include examples from every aspect of life: career, health, wealth, and leisure. Trust me when I tell you this simple exercise can change your life. It happened for me.

My Design for Living includes:

1. _____

2. _____

3. _____

4. _____

5. _____

6. _____

7. _____

8. _____

9. _____

10. _____

This exercise is available for download at www.businessofdesign.com/worksheets.

Section 2: The Power of a Personal Design for Living

 Let me share three incidents with you that occurred shortly after I prepared my own **Design for Living**.

ONE

Six years ago, my firm operated rent-free from an unused portion of my husband's office building. It wasn't a stylish looking destination so we decided not to put our name on the exterior of the building. However, the price was right and we had all the space we needed.

Under the guidance of my business coach Marysia Czarski, my staff created a group **Design for Living**, which focused on team dreams and goals. They agreed that the building did not match the **Kimberley Seldon Design Group** brand and determined we needed a new and improved space.

"Are you kidding me?" I thought. "This space is *free*. It's fine. Who cares?"

My mind was completely closed to the idea. But, a couple of months later a friend mentioned a lovely office space for sale up the street -- three floors with windows all around and seven parking spaces. I drove home past the building, wondering how I could ever afford it on our current income. But the prospect caused such excitement, the next day I phoned the listing agent for a tour. To my surprise, I made an immediate offer.

By spring, we moved in and by fall our income increased enough to carry the new expense effortlessly.

TWO

The second incident was equally dramatic. I met with nearly every single Canadian publisher to discuss a book on design, but none could afford to produce the book I envisioned. Shortly after identifying "writing a book" on my own **Design for Living**, I received an email from a US publisher. It took just one phone call to agree on a fee, an advance amount and a timeline for a new book called, "**500 Ideas for Small Spaces**". I wrote the book in six months and it was in bookstores in less than a year.

THREE

The third event involved champagne glasses I designed for the **Home Shopping Network (HSN)**. My partner and I worried we'd ordered too many and might be stuck with warehouses full of glasses after my on-air appearances. Joking that Oprah was our only hope, I added to my **Design for Living** list: "Get Oprah to promote champagne glasses." A few months later, someone at <u>O Magazine</u> called to say they saw the champagne glasses and wondered if I would like to feature them in the magazine?

When the January issue of Oprah arrived in early December (just in time for Christmas), imagine my surprise at finding a full-page endorsement heading Oprah's 'O List'. To this day, I have no idea how her people found out about the glasses, or who sent them a set for photography. Thank you, Oprah. Thank you, Universe.

> Soon after Oprah's endorsement we got a call from Tyra Banks & Co. who put my champagne glasses on their website.
>
> From there, we had an introduction to Ellen.
> And so on, and so on.

Ask for everything you want. Even if you don't know how it's going to happen.

I'm telling you there is no fairy godmother to grant you permission to enjoy 12 weeks vacation or work 30 hours a week or double your take home pay. If you are waiting for a sign to tell you it's ok to want more – then consider this book the sign!

Once your **Design for Living** is complete, you are on your way to creating a Mature Business.

Write your **Design for Living** immediately, don't delay. Do it now, even if it's not perfect. What I have found in teaching this course is that many of us are perfectionists. We want to "think about it" and come back to it when we can "do it perfectly." Trust me, the only way to do it right is to do it right now!

Put your personal Design for Living somewhere prominent.

My very own Design for Living

- Look at it every day.

- Let it be the yardstick by which you measure every decision.

- Use it as a catalyst to taking action and meeting deadlines.

In the next section we discuss the creation of an **Action Plan** to help you realize the items on your **Design for Living**.

****

Complete **Exercise #5: Design for Living** before moving on to the next section.

****

Section 3: Putting your Design for Living into Action

Action. It's great to have intentions, but if you don't put the new ideas into practice you will not get the results you desire. Now that you've completed a **Design for Living**, you'll want to follow it up immediately with an **Action Plan**.

When you review your **Design for Living** you'll find that some initiatives are relatively easy to achieve. But others may take a little more effort. On my first **Design for Living** list I jotted down "Work 5 days per week" instead of the 24/7 I'd been working until then. Because my clients had regular jobs, I thought I should work around their schedules, being available when it was convenient for them. Yes, this cut into my family time but I juggled, my husband did more than his fair share and we worked it out.

Imagine my surprise when I spent a day with John Saladino, a well-known New York interior designer and he told me I was actually doing the industry a disservice by running my business in this way. "Professional businesses," he said, "have regular hours. You wouldn't dream of asking a lawyer to meet you at 7 pm on Sunday evening because it was more convenient for you. Would any other professional work inconsistent hours? Of course not."

Establishing professional hours is easy to accomplish. Here's how to do it, right now:

1. List your new hours on your website, email and voice message.
2. Notify existing clients of the new hours.
3. Stick to them.

Done! You can check that off your list.

I thought my clients would flip out when I made this change and in truth, a couple did bristle, but they adapted. New clients, introduced to my regular hours from the outset, never question them. And I now looked – and felt -- more professional.

Some of your Design for Living entries may seem downright daunting:

- You want to be published in a magazine?

- Make guest appearances on a TV show?

- Increase your revenue by 100%?

- Write *the* definitive guide to decorating?

> The way to make these things happen is by developing an **Action Plan**.

Roll up your sleeves – but you're not going to work harder, you're going to work smarter. You can't just say I want to star in a TV show and expect it to happen. Producers typically don't come knocking on doors in the hopes that they will stumble across somebody who just happens to want a TV show! So your **Action Plan** might include developing a television story idea and pitching it to well known producers, appearing as a guest on existing television shows, taking a course in camera readiness, and appearing on stage at home shows.

In order to accomplish the items on your **Design for Living**, create an **Action Plan** by breaking each task into manageable steps. Let's see how it works.

Action Plan   **Desired Goal:**_____

Action	Next Steps	By When	Who

You will see the **Desired Goal** (objective) is listed at the top of the **Action Plan**.

- Column 1: Describe an **action**, which can help you reach your goal.

- Column 2: Identify specific **next steps** to help you accomplish the **action**.

  o Note: an **action** item may have 1 or 100 next steps beside it, depending on its complexity.

- Column 3: Provide a date **by when** the **next step** is to be completed or initiated.

  o Note: complex next steps may require both an initiation date and a completed by date. For example, it may take three weeks to research something, so the by when commitment should note both start and completion of the research.

- Column 4: In the **who** column, record the initials of the person responsible for completing the **next step**.

  o Note: your initials may figure heavily in this column or you may want to delegate certain tasks to staff, or enlist the help of friends and family who have specific expertise.

A detailed **Action Plan** provides clarity around your intentions and measures milestones towards success. If you only have 15 minutes to devote to a task on a given day, then do the 15 minutes. In my experience I rarely have to take every step on the **Action Plan**. At some point in the journey (and it might be anywhere) a door opens. You might make one phone call and somebody says, "Hey, I know precisely who you can speak to or how to make that happen quickly." With that one phone call you have just fast tracked beyond the first 12 items on your **Action Plan**! But if you didn't make that one phone call you would have missed it.

Remember, "**by when**" dates are non-negotiable. Build a realistic plan and stick to it.

A detailed *Action Plan* provides clarity around your intentions and measures milestones towards success.

Sample Action Plan

Let's say you want to purchase and flip a house for resale and profit. Your **Action Plan** might look like this:

Action Plan   **Desired Goal:** <u>Flip a House for Profit</u>

Action	Next Steps	By When	Who
Research costs	Research typical materials and renovation costs	Apr. 3	RT
Create savings plan	Start a savings plan	Apr. 3	KS
Find partner	Find a financial partner	May 10	KS
Develop basic understanding of construction	Take course at local college • Class starts • Class ends	Sept. 10 Dec. 5	KS
Research trades	Ask peers for reliable leads on trades	April 30	KS
Research suppliers	Prepare list of possible suppliers	April 30	RT
Find a realtor	Phone Jessica for recommendation	Apr. 1	KS
Find a realtor	Search websites for recommendations	Apr. 1	RT
Find a realtor	Begin interviewing perspective realtors	Apr. 10	KS
Find a realtor	Finalize choice of realtor	Apr. 21	KS
Create a budget	Ask David for help (accountant friend)	Apr. 3	KS
Create a budget	Put together first draft of budget	Apr. 12	KS
Secure financing	Make appointment with bank manager	Apr. 4	KS
Secure financing	Review first draft with bank manager	Apr. 15	KS
Secure financing	Secure financing	Apr. 20	KS
Create timeline	Prepare timeline to buy and sell home	May 15	KS

EXERCISE #6: Action Plan

Create an **Action Plan** directly from your own **Design for Living**. If you are stuck on which steps to take, ask for help – ideally from someone with expertise or interest in the required area. It's possible just requesting help with the **Action Plan** will elicit invaluable guidance. Use this page to create an **Action Plan** around one of the items on your **Design for Living**.

Action Plan   Desired Goal: _____

Action	Next Steps	By When	Who

This exercise is available for download at www.businessofdesign.com/worksheets.

Section 4: Building the Foundation for a Mature Business

 By completing your own **Design for Living** and **Action Plan** you are laying a foundation for your **Mature Business.** I repeat these exercises annually (or more frequently when necessary) and I have yet to be disappointed with the results.

While invaluable, your **Design for Living** and **Action Plan** are not enough to transform your business from **Infancy** or **Toddlerhood** into **Maturity.** There's still hard work to do, but I guarantee you will be amazed with the results if you incorporate the guidance suggested in the next chapter on **Process Management – Pathway to Satisfaction by Design.**

****

Complete **Exercise #6: Action Plan** for every item on your **Design for Living.**

****

Feeling lucky? Most optimists do. But you know what they say… the only sure thing about *luck* is - it will change!

If you're relying on luck, like I was, to complete client projects, the day will come where you will fail – and miserably. In **Chapter Four** we begin to build a system of **Satisfaction by Design**.

And… the day my business coach told me, "You sound like you've been drinking the "Designer Kool-Aid," and the two wake up calls that came next.

CHAPTER FOUR
Process Management
Pathway to Satisfaction by Design

In this Chapter

- Section 1: Creative People... and Why we Need Systems
- Section 2: Why Small Businesses Fail
- Section 3: The Big Mistake

Those of you with some business background are fortunate indeed. That knowledge is invaluable. But if you're like me, you have no formal business training. I compensated by hiring a business coach recommended by a friend whose business acumen I admired. When I asked Marysia Czarski (the prospective coach) how many design firms she had worked with in the past, she said: "Zero."

I laughed -- how on earth was she going to help me?

The work of a design firm is complex. Each project is unique, every client different, budgets and timelines difficult to determine with accuracy. I patiently explained to Marysia that I wasn't selling widgets or running a bank. As we talked, it was clear she wasn't grasping just how unique I was.

Our conversation continued; she telling me about her corporate coaching background and clients in banking, automotive and food distribution, and I telling her about the world of interior design. In her expert opinion I was running my operation with weak business practices when I should be running my firm along the lines of a bank or a Starbucks. Excuuuuuuse me? Don't you know who I think I am? I'm a designer, we're creative.

"The minute you take someone's hard-earned money, you are no longer a 'creative business' you are a 'business'."

Creative Business Kool-Aid

 Marysia said I sounded as if I'd been drinking the designer Kool-Aid. Thinking the fact I ran a "creative business" allowed me to ignore the rules that govern good business in general.

> "Forgive me for being blunt, but the minute you take someone's hard-earned money, you are no longer a 'creative business' you are a 'business.'"

In the past six years (and counting) I've worked regularly with Marysia and I now think of myself as a business person first and a creative person second. In fact, after careful analysis it turns out that twenty percent of my job is creative. The other eighty percent is all business.

20% Creative + 80% Business = The Interior Design Profession

Needless to say, I am very happy Marysia convinced me I needed her help. Over the years we've worked together she has doubled my revenue three times, steered me out of danger and kept me on target numerous occasions. She's taught me how to prepare budgets, hire staff and grow my business.

I cannot underestimate the value of turning to outside sources when you reach the limits of your expertise.

Section 1: Creative People... and Why we Need Systems

I mentioned earlier that I am concerned by what I see as a "mass dissatisfaction" with the design industry in general. And I believe inconsistency is responsible. When people hire a design firm they often have no idea what they are going to get, in terms of work process or fee structure. Even scarier, the design community seems to have no idea either. Most just make it up as they go along. This discrepancy creates worry in clients before a project even starts. I wonder how we can satisfy a client who is convinced before a project begins that we won't be able to make her happy?

If you know that a new client has had a bad experience in the past (and who hasn't?), then you must be aware of their concerns. You may have integrity, but a new client doesn't know that yet.

Show your clients from the first phone call that your firm is going to give them a different *experience* from others they have worked with in the past.

- Return phone calls and emails promptly.

- Answer questions *honestly*.

- Show up or call when you say you will.

- Provide honest time lines and costs - even if it's not what they want to hear.

> We earn our client's trust and respect one day at a time, by showing them a systematic approach to the process of design.

Systems create order out of chaos

You may be thinking… "I'm a creative person. I thrive on controlled chaos. It's part of my 'magic'," but I promise you, clients don't thrive on chaos and don't appreciate "magic." They want consistent, reliable results. Nor do trades, or staff, like disorder. And you may be surviving… but thriving?

I doubt it.

 An orderly business says to your customer, staff, trades and customers. **We know what we're doing.** We're experts. The rest of this industry may suffer from inconsistency, but we don't. We know how to get things done: on time, on budget, with consistently pleasing results. **We are a sure bet.**

Consistency is born of order.

> Order comes from working in a systematic fashion, anticipating common pitfalls and preparing the client, staff and trades for inevitable disruptions.

Once I stopped relying on "magic" and turned myself over to a systematic and structured set of procedures, I was able to:

- Consistently satisfy my clients.

- Benefit from regular referrals from clients.

- Experience rare conflicts with trades.

- Make far fewer costly errors.

- Complete projects on time and on budget.

- Have a staff that is extremely competent, consistently reliable and happier.

- Make more money.

- Love going to work.

 However, before I could accomplish this, I had to be convinced that "my way" wasn't working. Since Bitter, Angry, Resentful and Disappointed were becoming constant companions, I was willing to acknowledge there might be something I needed to learn. But what?

In a single day, I got two wake up calls.

ONE

The first one was a shock. My husband (who doesn't work for me, but was putting in many unpaid hours in accounting…) announced, "We are going to have to borrow money to pay staff this month." WHAT? How is that possible? We are working like crazy. Everybody is flat out busy. We are billing more hours than ever before. If you were in the room with me when that call came you would have heard me say, "Cash flow? What are you talking about?"

Sure, I had invoiced clients for billable hours, but I was so busy working I hadn't noticed how few actually paid their bills promptly. In fact, some owed as much as 6 months in back fees.

Can you relate?

 Cash Flow refers to money coming in and money going out. It's not complicated, but if you are spending more than you are collecting, you are going to have a cash flow problem.

I mistakenly took invoices sent to clients for money coming in and I soon discovered the two did not necessarily go hand-in-hand.

In addition to thousands of dollars in uncollected design fees, I also had a staff that had no limits on spending (because I hadn't given them any). When someone needed pens, we bought a gross. Graph paper? Let's buy a case. Stamps – enough to send Christmas cards to our clients for 10 years. Pretty pink file folders with flowers on them? Had to have 'em. So yes, of course I had a cash flow problem.

TWO

The second wake up call happened that same day as we were sitting in our weekly Topline meeting (Topline is a full staff meeting where we review in detail the status of every single client). As a design project is completed we provide our clients with a Client Binder, which is a reference guide to project details.

During Topline I would ask: "Who's going to produce Mrs. Smith's Client Binder?"

Somebody would volunteer but inevitably ask, "What's in the Client Binder again?"

"It includes paint chips, floor plans, fabric swatches, warranties, cleaning instructions, etc." Off this staff member would go and return to me during the week with the finished Client Binder. I'd review it -- because I had to have my hand in everything, it's my name on the door -- and of course, I found some ways to improve on what was presented to me. Again, I would send the designer off with changes to be made to the Client Binder. After several attempts at a finished product I would pronounce one ready to send out.

Next month, as we completed another project, we'd begin the entire process again. "What's in the binder?" "Let's see, I think it includes paint chips, floor plans, fabric swatches, warranties, cleaning instructions. Oh yeah, and I think we added the client's inspiration photos to the last one, should we put those in there too?" "Sure, good idea. Bring it to me in a few days and I'll take a look at it."

Only this time, a different staff member volunteered to produce the binder so this notebook didn't look anything like the last one and don't forget, I invested several hours in producing the last one. So we'd repeat the detailed back and forth and finally end up with something different – but acceptable.

I kid you not; this tiring scenario went on for a year. Finally, in the middle of this particular Topline meeting the penny dropped – I saw that this was never going to end. The dozens of hours we spent discussing and working on Client Binders was time wasted, hours that were not being billed, and time we could ill-afford when we were busy with clients.

I remembered what my business coach said:

"Without systems in place, you will make mistakes, run around in circles and eventually go mad or burn out."

By letting go of my old style of doing every task as if it were a custom assignment, I would be able to build a business based on *Satisfaction by Design*.

Satisfaction by Design: reliance on a systematic and structured set of procedures to complete projects on time, on budget, with consistently pleasing results.

At that moment, I asked a member of the design team to make a KSDG Client Binder Template. Just one binder - the idiot's guide to Client Binders - a pattern for making an endless number of binders that look exactly the same. Like a Starbucks Grande Latte – exactly the same, every time. This team member went on to produce a gorgeous binder with pre-printed tabs, corporate logo on the front, dividers with templates in place where fabric and paint chips are adhered, preprinted lines where written descriptions are required. Today, we have a shelf of empty KSDG Client Binders, waiting to be used.

So now Topline meetings sound like this when we finish a project:

Kimberley: "We've finished Mrs. J's house, she's really happy." (cheers all around)

KSDG staff: "I'll make the binder by Thursday and we'll send it to her on Friday when we deliver her thank you gift."

And then a wonderful, magical thing happens… I never hear another word about the Client Binder. I know it's being made to my exact standards, I know the client is going to receive it in a timely fashion and I know we have an exact copy which we keep in our office in case the client's copy is lost or damaged.

Creating systems is crucial if you want to thrive, which is way better than just surviving. It's possible to break every aspect of your business down into detailed procedures, like we did with our Client Binder and ultimately, with our collections and **Cash Flow** policies.

What's that you say? You're too busy?

If you are too busy to improve your systems for working, you will have plenty of time to spend with Bitter, Angry, Resentful and Disappointed.

Section 2: Why Small Businesses Fail

Entrepreneur and Business expert Michael E. Gerber is the author of "The E Myth Revisited, Why Most Small Businesses Don't Work and What to Do About It" (see e-myth. com and michaelegerber.com).

 Gerber sites one contributing factor to the failure rate of small businesses as: owners who are too busy working *in* the business to work *on* the business.

In other words, by staying in constant motion with tasks requiring immediate attention it's not possible to pay attention to or shape the business as a whole. So, you can be working, working, working and not realize cash flow has trickled to a drip, or costly advertising campaigns aren't producing effective results, or too many clients are not as happy as they might be.

Michael E. Gerber says the only way to break this cycle of non-stop work is to create systems to run the business and then teach people to run the systems.

Gerber's suggestions to standardize business (create systems) in order to increase profitability and manageability are shared by many business leaders.

McDonald's is often the gold standard of an orderly business model. The hamburgers are consistent each and every time regardless of which province, state or country you are visiting. That's because Ray Kroc, the creator of the McDonald's empire, worked *on* the business, not *in* the business. In other words, he didn't make a single hamburger or tie an apron around his waist. Instead, he created a system for making a very specific product – a McDonald's hamburger. The system was so detailed and specific any teenager could follow it and produce consistent results each and every time.

 If Ray Kroc had taught himself how to make McDonald's hamburgers, he would still be flipping burgers, cleaning the kitchen and restocking, and probably keeping company with our friends Bitter, Angry, Disappointed and Resentful.

"Wait a minute," you say. "I like making hamburgers (decorating homes, drafting floor plans, designing gardens, project managing new construction)."

That's ok, so do I. But I've narrowed my skill set to include the tasks I'm both very good at and love doing. Other responsibilities are delegated to competent staff members.

For a long time I looked orderly on the outside, and certainly tried hard to keep that appearance going. But it's not possible to just *appear* orderly; you actually have to *be* orderly.

 Initially, I resisted "systems" because each job is so different, each client is different. There is no way to systematize creativity, right? Wrong!

Once I introduced a system for managing **Cash Flow** and another for producing a **Client Binder,** positive changes were noticeable. I was eager to create systems for every aspect of my business.

And as I learned to systemize my business and delegate properly, I saw my staff enter a new level of confidence and professionalism. It was a thrilling time in my career -- and personal life because I finally had one.

Let's just agree that you might benefit from a few key systems. Where do you start? Oh, that's easy.

Section 3: Oops, the Big Mistake

 Have you ever made a mistake?

Sure, everyone has. Somewhere along the line you've disappointed a client, dropped the ball, or caused someone to complain.

As for big, stupid, humiliating and expensive blunders, I'll start with an example of my own.

The Big Blunder

A few years ago we were hired to do a small job for a repeat client, named Mrs. B. We'd decorated several rooms in her home and she called us back to renovate and redecorate her husband's office. We measured the room, designed a custom desk, and installed our new built-ins. The room was looking fabulous. So far, so good. But when the custom desk arrived… it would not fit into the room.

"What? How could it not fit in the room? I took the measurements myself."

In my office, the process for measuring a space is as follows: we (either a senior designer or I) measure the space and create an initial concept. We pass this information to a junior designer who prepares an AutoCAD drawing. At a glance, the floor plan looked fine. It was only after we'd made the costly mistake we discovered the junior designer had added the 12" depth of the new built-in bookshelves to the exterior of the room rather than the interior of the room – enlarging the room by one foot – on paper!

OOPS!

Since our policy is to pay for our mistakes we:

$$ Purchased the desk, which went into our inventory.

$$ Ordered a new desk in the correct size.

$$ Paid to remove the first desk and deliver the second desk.

$$ Ate crow with our client.

When I told the client how the error occurred, and explained that we would absorb the costs including the additional design hours and moving fees, she berated me: "How could you make a mistake like this, you've been in business so long?"

She was absolutely right. We should have had an adequate checkpoint in place.

 A system is born

From that day on, we have a new procedure at **Kimberley Seldon Design Group**. When measuring interiors and furniture, we always double-check the measurements with drawings in hand.

This is part of a corporate philosophy of **Satisfaction by Design**.

Now it's your turn...

To improve your business don't you have to at least acknowledge there is room for improvement?

EXERCISE #7: The Big Mistake

What was your biggest mistake? Write it down. Purge yourself of this embarrassing episode. Tell the most shamefully stupid, I-can't-believe-I-did-that moment you've had in business. Or better still - write them all down. If you have been in business for longer than a month, you've got some good stories to tell. List the blunders here.

1. _____
_____
_____

2. _____
_____
_____

3. _____
_____
_____

4. _____
_____
_____

5. _____
_____
_____

6. _____
_____
_____

7. _____
_____
_____

8. _____
_____
_____

This exercise is available for download at www.businessofdesign.com/worksheets.

I propose you don't follow my example. It took years of compounded mistakes before I was willing to hire a business coach and recognize the mess I had created.

 I wasn't alone, however -- here are some mistakes that students from Kimberley Seldon's Business of Design™ course have humbly shared:

Mistake	Cost	
Interior Designer: "I miscalculated the yardage for an upholstery order. When half the furniture was upholstered, the workroom realized they required more fabric. We tried to re-order additional fabric but unfortunately, it had been discontinued. Now, we had to order a different fabric in the total yardage. We also had to pay the upholsterer for doing part of the work twice."	Fabric Labour Lost fees **Total**	$ 12,700 $ 1,300 $ 2,600 $16,600
Commercial Designer: "For an office project we ordered twenty four boardroom chairs, clad in leather. The leather was ordered from Italy and because the timeline was tight we arranged for it to be sent directly to the upholstery shop. When the completed chairs arrived at the client's office, they were the wrong colour. In fact, they were pink… not tan."	Leather Labour Lost fees **Total**	$60,000 $36,000 $ 6,700 $102,700
Decorator: "I typed the wrong number on a sofa order and we didn't catch it until the wrong sofa arrived at the client's house, upholstered in her $400 per yard fabric."	New Fabric Labour Lost Fees **Total**	$ 8,800 $ 1,700 $ 3,200 $13,700
Stager: "I delivered all my furniture and product to clients who had not yet paid me a deposit. In addition, I did not have a signed contract. I never got paid despite the fact the client's house sold in less than 2 weeks."	Unpaid Invoices Lost Fees **Total**	$ 15,000 $ 4,000 $19,000

Mistake	Cost	
Architect: "I was behind in my work, so I asked a junior to prepare plans for a small bathroom reno. As the client meeting approached, I had no time to review the plans; reasoning I could acquaint myself with them once on site. Opening the drawings for the first time, I saw the client's bathroom had been enlarged, eliminating the walk in closet and the bedroom's existing fireplace. Since the client's hadn't asked for that, I lost the job."	Lost Fees **Total**	<u>$75,000</u> $75,000
Landscaper: "I built a pool on municipal property. We filed for bankruptcy."	**Total**	$$$$$

Everybody makes mistakes. How you handle them speaks volumes about your character and the integrity of your firm.

If I told you there was a way to eliminate the majority of mistakes you make, wouldn't that be appealing? Well, there is a way to accomplish just that… reliance on a system of **Satisfaction by Design** rather than the fallible system of *Satisfaction by Luck*.

Satisfaction by Design: reliance on a systematic and structured set of procedures to complete projects on time, on budget, with consistently pleasing results.

How to Grow Your Business

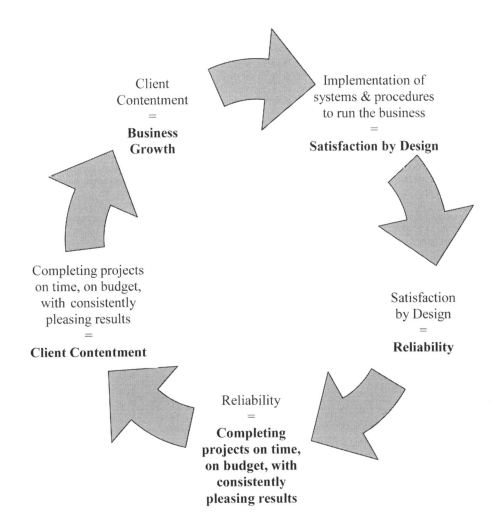

Client
Contentment
=
**Business
Growth**

Implementation of
systems & procedures
to run the business
=
Satisfaction by Design

Completing projects
on time, on budget,
with consistently
pleasing results
=
Client Contentment

Satisfaction
by Design
=
Reliability

Reliability
=
**Completing
projects on time,
on budget, with
consistently
pleasing results**

In **Chapter Five** we perform magic by turning 2 sentences into a business and life-changing statement. And, as if that were not enough, we show you how 1 system can save you dozens/hundreds/thousands of hours.

Want more life? Keep reading.

Oh yes, and most importantly, I'll tell you how I like my coffee.

Operations Manual

In this Chapter

- Section 1: Embracing a Mission Statement
- Section 2: Creating an Operations Manual
- Section 3: Learning to Delegate

Section 1: Embracing a Mission Statement

A **mission statement** is a short written announcement detailing a company's purpose and projecting its vision. It's often used as a guide to taking action and making decisions and it typically provides clients and staff with an overview of your company's core ideology.

If you're a small design firm or sole proprietor, you may be thinking, "What do I need that for"?

When my coach suggested I write my own mission statement my reaction was similar. Since it seemed important to *her*, I acquiesced and committed some thoughts to paper. In time, we honed our mission statement to read:

> **Kimberley Seldon Design Group Mission Statement:**
>
> At KSDG we strive to serve our valued and respected clientele through a system of **Satisfaction by Design**. We rely on experience, expertise and impeccable integrity to complete projects on time, on budget, with consistently pleasing results.

In two sentences our Mission Statement reminds me:

- To follow the procedures I've developed over two decades - thus avoiding a tempting short cut which nearly always leads to problems.
- To value my own experience and expertise.
- To respect my commitment to impeccable integrity.
- To respect my clients, especially when it comes to money and timing.

Wow! Just two sentences.

EXERCISE #8: Mission Statement

A mission statement is your company's goal and core ideology. To arrive at your own mission statement, answer the following questions.

1. Why did you start your business?

2. What level of service do you provide?

3. What motivates you and your employees?

4. How do you differentiate yourself from the competition?

5. Who are your customers?

Next, brainstorm these loose ideas and explore linking various thoughts.

For example - if you said:

- I started my business in order to provide clients with functional and stunning interiors.

- I provide clients with exceptional, efficient service.

- I differentiate myself from the competition by living up to my word/promise at all times.

Your Mission Statement might read:

At _____, our mission is to lead – never follow – our competition. We do this by providing exceptional and efficient service, culminating in functional and stunning interiors throughout North America.

Now, it's your turn.

In the space below, summarize all of your goals into 1-3 short sentences. Keep it brief - short enough that clients remember it, but long enough to communicate your ideals.

Mission Statement

_____

_____

_____

_____

_____

_____

_____

This exercise is available for download at www.businessofdesign.com/worksheets.

I think of our *Operations Manual* as the "idiot's guide" to working at KSDG.

Section 2: Creating an Operations Manual

In the previous chapter we discuss how easy it is to make mistakes. However, an error - while unpleasant - can provide you with the momentum needed to create systems that will help you achieve greater results in future. Once those systems or procedures are committed to paper, they earn a permanent place of honor in the **Operations Manual**.

I think of our **Operations Manual** as the "idiot's guide" to working at **KSDG**. Over the years, I've learned that nearly every task we perform can be distilled into a simple process. With step-by-step instruction available to all employees, I am rarely asked to answer operational questions, something that used to take up a lot of my time.

Some pages review standard direction for issues such as Internet policy, sick days, dress codes, etc. Other pages are customized to suit our unique environment. How customized? Well, one of my favourite pages contains instructions for how each of us likes his/her coffee.

We often take turns running out for coffee. One staff member noticed it took considerable time to explain what each person wanted to drink, although most had the same order daily. So we devised a page in our **Operations Manual** that looks like this:

SECTION 2: General Office	**POLICY #:** 1234
TOPIC: Coffee Time	
BY: Cheryl Horne	**PAGE:** 1 of 1
AUTHORIZATION SIGNATURE:	
Kimberley's Coffee: Medium, non-fat, extra hot latte Splash of whole milk, sprinkle of cocoa powder	
Bret's Tea: Large cup, Orange Pekoe Whole milk, tea bag in	
Erin's Coffee: Medium non-fat, mochachino Half the sweetness	

Believe it or not, it's a real time saver. In fact, it works so well, we've added our favourite salads and sandwiches to the page.

Another simple example is our policy on returning phone calls and emails. At **KSDG** our policy is to return every weekday phone call and email within 24 hours, no exceptions. That does not mean we have an answer to the question (since an accurate answer may take longer), it just means acknowledging the message and providing the client with a time line for getting back with an answer. For example, "Mrs. Jones, thank you for your message. I understand you would like to push the painting schedule back by two weeks. I have a call into my painter now and I hope to hear from him by tomorrow with an answer to that question. **I will phone you by end of day tomorrow.**"

> **"I will phone you by end of day tomorrow."** *This is a promise* - a firm commitment.

Our **Operations Manual** backs up this policy as follows:

SECTION 2: General Office	POLICY #: 12345
TOPIC: Returning Calls and Emails	
BY: Aysun Kuck	PAGE: 1 of 1
AUTHORIZATION SIGNATURE:	

At **KSDG** our commitment to clients includes:
- Returning phone calls and emails within 24-hours (assume business day).
- If you do not have an answer for the customer, acknowledge receipt of email or phone call and advise as to **by when** you will have the information.
- Follow up promptly (as promised) with the customer.

Any task, from the simplest to the most complex can be clearly defined on paper. Here are some other tasks captured in our **Operations Manual**:

- Answering the phone

- Enrolling a client for design project or consultation

- Preparing the Client Binder

- Logging billable hours

- Obtaining written quotes from trades

- Building a custom cabinet

- Preparing a tracking sheet

- Preparing a worksheet

Originally I thought introducing systems would mean the end of creativity, but I found the opposite to be true. These simple procedures save time, eliminate needless stress, and provide my staff and me with additional time for creative assignments.

Employees tell me they are happier with systems in place – in part because they know what it takes to get the job done and please the boss.

Imagine volunteering to create the Client Binder and the boss sending you back to your desk to make improvements five times. Pretty discouraging. Or, being a new employee and needing to ask a question you know has been answered three times. Instead, open the **Operations Manual** and follow the step-by-step guidance.

If you have staff, imagine how helpful it is to hand them an **Operations Manual** and provide them with the exact steps to doing a specific task. Training a new employee becomes a simple and straightforward procedure. When someone's on vacation, any staff member is able to pick up the thread of a project and keep the job moving forward.

I once had a good employee who liked to keep everything in her head, but when she was out of the office, the rest of us had a terrible time finding even basic information. If she was away sick or on vacation client questions caused panic while we scrambled to come up with an answer.

> Having systems sends a message to clients (and trades and staff) that I am orderly, I am in charge, things are running according to plan and I am managing all details well. I never want my clients to worry about project details. I want them to know, beyond a shadow of a doubt, that I am managing that for them.

The following sample is a page out of the **KSDG Operations Manual** that relates directly to the story I shared earlier about measuring twice before approving any drawing.

SECTION 5:	Interior Design	POLICY #: 2345
TOPIC:	Obtaining Trade Day Measurements - Measure Twice, Build Once	
BY:	Bret Tinson	PAGE: 1 of 1
AUTHORIZATION SIGNATURE:		

Trade Day is intended to kick-start the client's design or renovation project in an effective and efficient manner (**Trade Day** is reviewed in **Kimberley Seldon's Business of Design**™: **Part 2**). One important task for **Trade Day** involves obtaining initial measurements of the client's home for the purposes of creating accurate floor plans, elevations, or technical drawings.

KSDG Staff on site at Trade Day:

- Take measurements of walls, windows, doors, ceiling heights, bulkheads, valances, columns and pillars; include elevation heights.

- Notations on floor and wall vents, alarms and light switches, cable and telephone access, radiators, baseboards, crown molding and door swings.

- Take measurements of light fixtures, including height AFF (above finished floor). Note electrical function including switching for lights (note door swings).

- Measure for reflected ceiling plan, including lighting, audio equipment, vents, etc.

- Take inventory and measurements for all existing furniture, plus any items that will be repurposed into the renovated/redecorated space.

- Take digital images of all areas – floors, walls and ceilings.

KSDG Staff upon return to office:

- Original plans to be copied with extra set placed in **Client Binder.**

- Transfer notes to AutoCAD drawings as directed by Senior Designer.

- All floor plans are to be prepared on standard **KSDG** title block.

- NOTE: **KSDG** is not responsible for Trade Measurements; each trade is responsible for taking his/her own accurate dimensions. However, **KSDG** takes its own measurements for purposes of accuracy and management. **Never provide measurements to trades**.

- Pass completed drawings to Senior or Intermediate for review.

- **Once drawings are approved, staff member returns to site to double check accuracy of drawings against site conditions.**

- After second site visit, drawings are labeled "approved" and put on shared drive.

Of course, you don't have to wait for a mistake to occur before creating a procedure for getting a task accomplished. The Client Binder epiphany I described previously provides a good example of a procedure that was created in order to simplify an oft-repeated task.

Another frequent task in our office involves receiving, approving and shipping fabric on behalf of clients. On the following page are the steps to achieving this procedure as identified in our **Operations Manual**.

SECTION 5: Interior Design	POLICY #: 4567
TOPIC: Fulfillment Room Fabrics - Tagging Fabrics	
BY: Kathy Seale	PAGE: 1 of 3
AUTHORIZATION SIGNATURE:	

Fabric ordered for clients arrives periodically at **KSDG** and must be stored in the Fulfillment Room (area where inventory is catalogued and held) until ready for shipping. The Finance Administrator is responsible for receiving, tagging and shipping COM (customer's own material) fabrics and trims to the workroom fabricating the furniture, drapery, etc.

When fabric/trim is received, these steps must be followed:

1: Check paperwork on roll/package to obtain our PO number and tag (client) name.

2: Open the tracking form (located on the shared drive > Interior Design Clients > Tracking Forms) and note location fabric/trim is to be shipped to and the corresponding PO # for workroom. Enter the shipping date on the tracking form and highlight it to show it's been completed. If fabric is not shipping out immediately, tag it as Received by noting "In Fulfillment Room" on tracking form, but do not highlight until it is shipped.

3: Pull fabric/ trim PO from client file located in the Finance Administrator's hardcopy files and confirm item name and quantity. Staple paperwork received from the bolt of fabric to this PO.
The CFA (cutting for approval) will be attached to our PO for fabric. There is generally no CFA for trims.

4: Open top of fabric roll or trim package and ensure that it matches the CFA.

5: Create a Tag Sheet to label the fabric for future use. The Tag Sheet template is found on the shared drive > Finance Administrator Files > Tag Sheet for fulfillment room). Fill in the workroom's PO # *found on the tracking form* and complete all other sections of the Tag Sheet. Add any special instructions to the sheet – e.g. "cut railroaded". When there are special instructions keep a copy of the Tag Sheet with our PO.

6: Print Tag Sheet.

7: Cut a small clipping of the CFA (or small piece from the roll/ trim if a CFA is not available) and staple it to the outlined box on the Tag Sheet (2" x 2").

8: Reseal packaging, insert Tag Sheet in plastic protector and tape to outside of roll/package.

9: Call courier to deliver fabric to appropriate workroom or hold in Fulfillment Room until required.

Room	Inv.#	PO	Product	Qty	Supplier	Date Ordered	ETA	Date Rec'd	Date Shipped
Dining	8295	5369	Bench fabric FD 561 gray stripe	5	ABC	Jun 8/09		Jul 12/09	
Dining	8295	5369	Bench pillow fabric	3	XYZ	Jun 8/09	Aug 1/09		
Dining	8295	5369	Bench pillow trim	4	123	Jun 8/09	Sept 2/09		

Kimberley Seldon

DESIGN GROUP

Date: _____

To: (Supplier)

Attn: (Contact Name)

From: Linda Jennings ext. 224

Client: (Client Last Name)

P O: (Purchase Order Number)

Tag: (Client Last Name and Product Name)

Notes:

(Fabric Name, Fabric Supplier, and
Yardage of Fabric Bolt)

FABRIC/TRIM SAMPLE

Section 3: Learning to Delegate

Once your business practice includes easy-to-follow systems, you are in a position to delegate – and achieve results.

 Prior to the Client Binder standardization, I lived by the adage – if you want something done right, do it yourself. On the rare occasion I did delegate, it didn't work – me grumbling about having to "fix" everything, and employees likely feeling frustrated and unmotivated.

When a business is mature, delegating frees you from smaller or mundane tasks to work on the more pressing matters. This hierarchy of tasks benefits the client as well, since delegated tasks are billed at a lower hourly rate.

"But, it's my name on the door. I have to make sure everything is done right," you say. Yes, you do have to make sure it's done right. **So define goals and clearly outline -- in writing -- the necessary steps to achieve the desired goal.** Create a precise procedure for each task, then others can follow the steps and produce results as good, or better, than yours.

Some aspects of business seem to demand a system or procedure, but others crop up out of mistakes. In **Chapter 7, Section 2: Taking Inventory,** I'll review the benefits of a thorough stocktaking that illuminates recurring issues. And we'll discuss the creation of procedures designed to eliminate the problems.

Author's Side Note:

The task of writing the **Operations Manual** seemed enormous to me and I wasn't really sure where to start. I decided to list it on my **Design for Living**.

Months went by and one day I received a phone call from Make a Wish Foundation, which grants wishes of children with serious medical conditions. A little girl asked for a bedroom makeover and they wondered if I would be willing to help. Absolutely!

In the middle of this project the case worker and I had a chance to spend some time together. I knew that Make a Wish wasn't a full-time occupation for her and I asked her what she did in addition to this valuable work. She told me she wrote operations manuals for companies. Needless to say, she was so appreciative of our willingness to provide this little girl's bedroom; she gave us the first 100 pages of our **Operations Manual** and provided a template for us to complete the rest. Don't ask questions; just put everything you can think of on your **Design for Living**.

Let's talk clients in **Chapter Six**.

1.   Is it possible to make them happy? Yes.

2.   How? By relying on a system of **Satisfaction by Design** rather than a system of *Satisfaction by Luck*.

3.   Is it that easy? Yes.

But watch out for sparks – if ignored, they'll send your client relationships up in smoke.

CHAPTER SIX
Client Insight and Contentment

In this Chapter

- Section 1: Caring for Clients
- Section 2: Satisfaction by Design
- Section 3: Ignore the Spark and Get Burned
- Section 4: Choosing the Right Clients

Shall we talk about clients? I know. Now you are wondering if I'm crazy! How could I possibly write a book that talks about clients when I'm still a practicing designer? After all, you're thinking, I must agree with you that clients are the ultimate thorn in the side, don't I? Isn't it every designer's favourite joke, "I love my job, if only it didn't involve clients" (eyes rolling in mock jest). Ha, ha, ha. Aren't we funny?

No, not really.

Don't for a minute think there is a way to justify this type of chronic, hateful thinking. It's bad for you, it's bad for the industry as a whole and it's unfairly directed at the very group of people that keep us all in business.

What's that you say? Your clients are extremely difficult, totally unreasonable and impossible to please. Hmmmmm. At some point, when I'd had more than a few "extremely difficult clients," I had to face the truth and investigate the common denominator... *me*.

Section 1: Caring for Clients

> ## Is it possible that everything "wrong" with your clients may be your own fault?

Is it possible that somehow you have not provided the client with sufficient reason to relax and trust you? That reliance on *luck* has failed? As difficult as it was to admit, this was true in my case. I wasn't *trying* to neglect clients. In fact, I wanted very much to please them. Yet, I had to admit there were too many instances where they were not pleased. Blaming the client may allow you to ignore your part in the breakdown by focusing on someone else's behaviour, but it also robs you of the most valuable opportunity you'll ever have to improve your business practices.

 My coach's suggestion helped me get past this blame game. She proposed I assume the client was right and I was wrong whenever there was a complaint or problem.

What? Let me repeat that.

My business coach proposed I assume the client was right and I was wrong whenever there was a complaint or problem.

Instead of wasting time "defending" myself, I listened carefully to the conflict. I was surprised to learn the client had some legitimate concerns. **Putting myself in the client's position allowed me to see how exasperating the process of renovation or decorating might have been for them.**

This new information allowed me to identify where my business practices needed improvement. Through the process, I gained powerful motivation to work *on* my business. I understood the need for a system that produced **Satisfaction by Design** so I could retire my faulty system of *Satisfaction by Luck*.

Over time, something miraculous occurred - my clients became reasonable, likeable, friendly people, from start to finish of the project. They trusted me when I said things were under control. We spoke with mutual respect. When a frustration occurred, I assessed where I might have made a better choice, taken a more decisive action or circumvented a problem. Soon, I was going to extra lengths to make these nice people happy. Instead of criticizing them I was actually enjoying the experience of working with them.

The clients, for their part, held my company to exacting performance standards, which ultimately served me well as a business owner. In time I developed real relationships with clients, attending family weddings and corporate cocktail parties. It wasn't long until I loved my work again.

When teaching **Kimberley Seldon's Business of Design**™ it is rare to meet a student who is not playing the blame game. They frequently remark that the client just "doesn't understand" – how difficult the job is, how much effort and time it requires, how hard the designer is working, etc. They'll express frustration because the client just 'doesn't get it.'

Is it possible a client doesn't "get it" because we haven't explained it well? Remember, the client is paying *you*; it's your job to make sure the customer is aware of the Who, What, When, How and How Much of a project at all times. The last thing you want is a client worrying about process.

Systems and procedures allow you to manage the client's expectations and instill a sense of calm and order to the project.

Section 2: Satisfaction by Design

 Satisfaction by Design ensures there is a system in place for managing the expectations of clients and anyone else associated with a project (staff and trades). Since we are no longer relying on *luck*, we know the development won't happen spontaneously. It has to be an integral part of procedural process leading to a successful finish.

If you haven't used this "management" muscle before, it may feel awkward and alien. But in time it becomes a fundamental part of your business practices.

How do you know if you are managing client expectations successfully?

At **KSDG** we have a simple measure: if the client contacts us – by phone, email, or text – to inquire about the status of their project, then we have failed. You may not mind clients contacting you, but it's not about *minding,* it's about acknowledging the client didn't know what was happening next, or why. Because if they had known what was happening next, they wouldn't have had to contact you. Somehow, something was missed.

The goal in our office is to make sure the client knows exactly **Who, What, When, How** and **How Much** at all times. If they need to call us to ask a question about project status, someone has dropped the ball. My staff knows my expectations around this because they are clearly outlined in our **Operations Manual**. If I meet with a staff member and say, "Mrs. C phoned me to find out where her (fill in the blank) is", that staff member knows I am not amused.

It's not that I don't want to speak with Mrs. C. In fact, I do want to speak with Mrs. C, but not to field a concern that would have been circumvented with proper communication.

 If you rely on *Satisfaction by Luck*, client expectations will not be met. And if you fail to manage expectations, you'll fail to please your clients. If you fail to please your clients, you'll experience constant frustration. If it doesn't improve, the job will be fraught with upset or you may be fired. It's almost always that simple.

> The number one reason any design professional is fired...
> the client's expectations were not managed.

Perhaps you were not dependable; you didn't show up when you said you would, didn't follow through or provide the necessary coaching. Maybe you assumed the client knew how the project would work, recognized there are always challenges on a job site, understood how billable hours worked, realized the project wasn't going to finish on time or on budget. I could add to this list ad infinitum.

Section 3: Ignore the Spark and Get Burned

If a client relationship begins to break down in some way, I can almost always point to the place where I didn't do my job well. It might be a moment where I strayed from procedure, or agreed to something I didn't have sufficient information about, a question I should have answered more thoroughly, or an off-hand comment that seemed easier to ignore than deal with directly. I call these *sparks* (more about sparks in a moment).

Today, I take full responsibility when a relationship gets off track. It is no longer the client's fault. It is my fault. By taking ownership, I can usually eliminate most of the difficulties, because the majority of clients are reasonable and decent. They want me to succeed.

Do we do this perfectly? Well, no.

Last year we were hired for a second project by a client we all adore. We decorated most of her waterfront condo, except the bathrooms, two years ago. Since she and her husband were going to Europe for the summer, she asked us to complete the two bathrooms while they were away. "No problem," I said.

Interesting response, no? I mean -- **have you ever been involved with a renovation project that was *no problem?***

When I spoke with the contractor he informed me he couldn't start the project until the end of July, but since it was a "simple" job, he could complete it quickly once started. Since my client was easygoing and already in Europe, I decided not to bother her with the details. I would instead push the contractor to work quickly and get the job done.

"If we're lucky," I thought, "we'll get it done in the nick of time."

> # Armed with my *Satisfaction by Luck* fantasy, things didn't go smoothly.

Unforeseen snags caused the project to fall farther behind. To compound the problem, the contractor got behind on his other projects, which impacted our progress. So instead of being finished, we were not even close when the clients returned from holidays.

 If only I had picked up the phone to let them know the status of the work, I could have prevented disappointment. But I fell back on old habits -- work harder, pester the contractor every day, be on site to make sure he keeps the work moving forward.

Because my client is very straightforward, she told me candidly why I had disappointed her. It was one of the saddest days I've ever experienced in my career. After all, I love this client. She is the last person I would want to disappoint. Yet, I am so grateful for her candor. I hope I never forget the look on her face as she shared her disappointment with me. I owe her a debt of gratitude and so do my future clients. She and I are working on our third project and I've learned my lesson – no more *Satisfaction by Luck*. Instead I will trust the systems and procedures I've created to bring every project to its successful completion.

If you're like me, you may find your tendency to want to please the clients or provide the answer they want to hear impedes your ability to manage expectations effectively.

Let me give you an example.

If a client asks, "When will the project be done? My children are coming home for Christmas and I want the house to be ready for their visit." Of course you want it to be done by Christmas. You want to make the client happy. However, it's September 1st and you know it is nearly impossible for the work to be completed in the timeframe requested. Still, you find yourself nodding your head:

Designer Says: That timeline is really tight, but we will do the best we can.

Client Hears: YES! I promise.

This might be followed with a 30-minute discussion about how hard it's going to be to meet the timeline, the large scope of work, logistical and coordination issues, inventory delays, holiday disruptions, etc. But the client only remembers: YES! I promise.

I've seen the above scenario a hundred times. Why should the client worry about project concerns? That's one of the things they are paying you for. They are also paying you to be honest with them, to have impeccable integrity and to treat them as the highest priority.

So rewind to the question posed earlier by the client.

Client Says: When will the project be done? My children are coming home for Christmas and I want it to be ready for their visit.

Designer Says: No. We cannot realistically be ready for Christmas. I'll tell you why.

Client Hears: No.

Designer Says: However, this is what we can have ready for Christmas. We can have the childrens' bedrooms painted and the family room redecorated. Perhaps we should put off beginning the kitchen renovation until January 5th so you can enjoy the holidays without disruption.

Client Hears: The children's bedrooms and family room will be ready for Christmas (I'm disappointed, because I want it all done, but at least some of it will be ready).

Now, watch what happens when a *spark* (an off hand comment that seems easier to ignore than deal with directly) is thrown:

Client Spark: Well, you're such a pro, I bet you will surprise me and have it all done by Christmas. LOL

Designer Says   Ha ha ha. You're right, I'm a miracle worker aren't I?

Client Hears: Yeah! I just may be able to have it all done before Christmas.

Rewind to the initial moment where the *spark* is thrown:

Client Spark: Well, you're such a pro, I bet you will surprise me and have it all done by Christmas. LOL

Designer Says: No. We cannot be ready for Christmas. Logistically, it's not possible.

Client Hears: No. It will not be fully completed by Christmas.

Can you see the difference? Sparks are sometimes subtle, but they are a powerful foe. I have the option to pretend I didn't understand the question (or see the *spark*), but if I choose to ignore it, a roaring fire may develop in its place. A *spark* such as, "I'm sure you'll have it ready for Christmas anyway, right?" needs an immediate response. "No. This project will not be ready for Christmas."

I've made the mistake of ignoring *sparks* in the past and it always goes badly.

I once had a client who jokingly said that I could choose anything I wanted for his home, provided the full budget remained at $50,000. The problem was, we were well into the project and the budget was *already* over $50,000. We both knew that. He was just joking. We had talked about the budget on several occasions and the client seemed very comfortable with the choices and decisions in progress. Since he was joking, I laughed along with his $50,000 remark and did not address the comment.

When the bills came in at $65,000 the client wondered if I had taken advantage. I felt miserable because I remembered the *"spark"* and knew if I had dealt with it right then, there would have been no reason for disappointment at the end of the project. In the end, we worked through the misunderstanding and the client agreed that he was pleased with the final result. I was fortunate, but it was yet another example of *Satisfaction by Luck*, rather than **Satisfaction by Design**.

Here's another example.

We had a longstanding client who was hosting a party for an exclusive event. At 2 pm on Friday afternoon the client phoned, "I'm having a party with a celebrity guest tomorrow at 6 pm and I need some help." Because he was a good client and we enjoyed working together I was happy to jump in at the last minute, despite my weekend plans.

I mobilized available staff and we swarmed the house in preparation for the party. There was a lot of work to do and a short amount of time to get it done. An outdoor tent required seating for thirty people. Planters and greenery were needed around the pool area. The house required fresh flowers and the usual pre-party fluffing. In addition, the client had forgotten to hire live music or purchase a gift for the visiting celebrity. At 4:30 on a Friday afternoon we were on the phone and in the shops getting the work done.

This was a dream job. I loved the speed of work and the nearly instant gratification. My staff enjoyed the challenge as well, since we rarely worked weekends or found ourselves in "emergency" situations. It tested our skills.

Things went off beautifully and as we reviewed the finished project with the client he thanked us profusely and then made an off-hand remark about how I would do anything for money.

A joke. A spark.

I really wanted to ignore that remark because I respected this client and I knew he was half-joking. But I turned gently towards him and said, "Mr. D, did you really mean that? We just gave up our Friday night and Saturday to take on this fun but challenging assignment. I think you are pleased with the results. Do you really believe I did this solely for the money?" The client was apologetic and assured me he was very pleased with the work. Mr. D and I never had another conversation like that again – and it wasn't the last time he gave us a challenging assignment. By dealing with that small *spark*, I believe I prevented a major fire from engulfing our relationship.

None of us likes to have those conversations with clients. It's easier, at least initially, to ignore an off-hand remark. Putting the sparks out as they occur takes discipline, but it speaks to your integrity as the owner of the company. In my experience, clients respect the fact that you are willing to check in with their comfort level and make sure you are providing them with the service they want and expect.

Of course, you also want to make sure you are *choosing* the right clients to begin with. Choosing clients? "Wait a minute," you're wondering, "don't they choose us?" Well, yes and no.

Section 4: Choosing Clients

By now, I hope you agree that it's possible to satisfy most (if not all) of your clients by managing expectations through a system of **Satisfaction by Design**. Choosing the right clients is part of the process.

When a potential client phones your office to inquire about services, of course they are interviewing you. That's expected and you want to make sure you can succinctly identify the services you provide and outline what sets you apart from the competition. You want to "close the deal" as they say. However, you also want to determine whether or not you are the right person/firm to satisfy this particular client's needs.

Is the potential client looking for someone to produce a particular style that's part of your repertoire? Is the timeline achievable, is the budget sufficient, or are there parameters such as travel, which might make the project difficult for you? Some basic fact gathering occurs initially. From there, you want to look for "red flags" -- warning signs that make this particular project seem doomed from the start.

Red flags can be subtle or obvious.

Potential Client: I've worked with twelve designers in the past and they were all incompetent.

Potential Client: My husband is cheap; I am going to have to sneak this past him.

Potential Client: I know it's November, but I must have a new kitchen in time for Christmas.

Potential Client: I've met other designers and their fees are lower than yours. I want a discount.

Potential Client: I would like to be your assistant during the project; I've always wanted to be a designer.

Potential Client: I'm a screamer, but I don't mean anything by it. You'll get used to me. I'm just passionate.

None of these things is necessarily a deal breaker, but it's important information going into a new job. Let's say you are ultra busy with 20 projects on the go and you simply cannot handle any new clients at the moment. In this case, turning down the wrong client will be easy.

However, if you are not working at capacity or you're just growing your business, it may be difficult to walk away from *any* client. In that case, consider the cost working with the wrong client. Are you prepared to work with a couple that does not see eye to eye on financing or end results? Can you comfortably endure sleepless nights when working around an aggressive, bullying customer? What about staff? How does the wrong client impact their view of working for you?

Here's an example of working with the wrong client.

My first meeting with Mr. G was classic. I arrived at his office for our initial meeting and I hear screaming, "Where's my freaking heart monitor?". I'm escorted into the very office where the screams are coming from and I can literally see the veins bulging on this man's neck. I'm no doctor, but I'm pretty sure this is not healthy heart behaviour.

He greets me warmly, and then returns to several more minutes of yelling at his frightened administrator. He explains that he's training for an athletic event and he must find his heart monitor before he leaves the office for the day. We begin our meeting and Mr. G describes a fabulous project. I already know I need to walk away and never look back. But, I'm human and I *want this job.* I begin to justify his behaviour and I tell myself, "He is under a lot of pressure. We'll take great care of him. I can handle this."

I accept the project and in fact, we get along quite well with Mr. G. We rely on a system of **Satisfaction by Design** and he is very reasonable with us at every stage.

Unfortunately, his contractor doesn't fare so well. Mr. G had already retained a contractor and we are introduced to him before our work begins. The contractor is a good guy, but he is somewhat inexperienced and his contract is sorely lacking in detail. Mr. G takes advantage of every weakness and makes the contractor's life – and that of his employees – miserable. Mr. G never screamed at anyone from my office, but we were subjected to weekly meetings where the contractor and his team were wildly abused and humiliated. It was a difficult project to enjoy with so much stress occurring on a regular basis.

Before you accept a project with the wrong client, consider the cost:

- Health, morale and confidence erode

- Brand and reputation may be tarnished

- Time and money are lost

Identify the types of clients your business is capable of satisfying and work hard to gain their trust. You will be rewarded with repeat business and referrals. More importantly, you will learn to love your job again. I know because it happened for me and it can happen for you.

> **Note:** I finished this initial project for **Mr. G.** but turned down further projects, which he offered to me. My staff took me to lunch to say: "Thank you."

In **Chapter Seven**: If you want to be happy for the rest of your working life then give your resources - trades, sub-trades, suppliers and manufacturers – clear, precise, written instructions for making you happy.

It couldn't be simpler. But I can't promise it's going to be easy.

And, it's time to hold tryouts for the "A" **Team**.

CHAPTER SEVEN
Resource Management

In this Chapter

- Section 1: Getting the Job Done Right
- Section 2: Taking Inventory
- Section 3: Growing the Operations Manual
- Section 4: Building the "A" Team
- Section 5: Resource Guide to Excellence (RGE)
- Section 6: Better Trade Relations

"It takes a village," is the phrase I think of when I'm pulling a team together to complete a client project. Every design practice, from sole proprietorships to multi-employee operations, relies on the experience, strength and talent of others to complete even the smallest projects.

Managing those individuals is a big task -- done well, projects get finished on time, on budget, with consistently pleasing results. Done poorly, projects may initially run smoothly, but before long you "hit a few snags."

Next, a bigger problem erupts and accusations fly; trades are pointing fingers. The client catches wind of "issues" and begins to worry about job site details then, overall progress. Soon the client feels resentful, after all isn't she paying you to do the worrying? In short order, the client begins to complain and... you know the rest. It's predictable.

What *should* be predictable is a project's success, not its total breakdown.

These problems can be avoided, but not by:

- Working more hours; being on call 24/7

- Working faster; rushing or cutting corners

- Applying more pressure to suppliers and trades; begging or bribing

- Settling for "good enough" due to time or budget constraints

- Doing everything personally

- Accusing clients of needing a psychiatric evaluation

Project difficulties cannot be corrected or eliminated by applying the same methods that created the problems in the first place. The old thinking – it's someone else's fault, if you want something done right then do it yourself, everything will be fine as soon as I finish _____ - won't take your business to a new level of excellence.

Creating a system of
Satisfaction by Design…

is the key to transforming
your business and your
life.

Section 1: Getting the Job Done Right

Defining project and corporate goals

Let's kick this section off by coming up with a definition for "**Getting the Job Done Right.**" What specifically does that mean?

 Describe in detail what achieving that ideal for each and every client would look like -- happy clients, repeat business, glossy photos for your website?

Everything is possible, so be thorough when creating this list of goals. For example, wouldn't "**Getting the Job Done Right**" allow you to charge more for your services? Of course. I have yet to meet a client who is not willing to pay for expertise. If you could make good on your promise to get the job done, on time, on budget, with consistently pleasing results each and every time, wouldn't that increase your value to all clients? Include thoughts on earning money, enjoying vacation time, recognition and publicity within your community or country, gaining repeat or referral clients.

The following are samples of potential targets/goals for "**Getting the Job Done Right.**"

1. Client is pleased with service and progress throughout the project.
2. Client refers new customers at the end of project.
3. Increased profits.
4. Vacation time is enjoyed without interruption.
5. Photography occurs at project end; photos added to website.
6. Publish project(s) in a design magazine.
7. Finished space is gorgeous and client is happy with every detail.
8. Regular and consistent positive feedback from client during project.
9. Regular and consistent positive feedback from trades and suppliers.
10. Deficiencies are completed in timely fashion; client never worries.
11. Trades works harmoniously together for the client's wellbeing.
12. Better (more prestigious) projects offered to us.
13. Agreement with client regarding budget and timing.
14. Staff more fulfilled and happier; less overall stress.
15. Clients pay invoices in timely manner; no arguing about money.

EXERCISE #9: Getting the Job Done Right

Now it's your turn. List every goal you can think of that would be the result of "**Getting the Job Done Right.**"

1. _____
2. _____
3. _____
4. _____
5. _____
6. _____
7. _____
8. _____
9. _____
10. _____
11. _____
12. _____
13. _____
14. _____
15. _____

This exercise is available for download at www.businessofdesign.com/worksheets.

****

Complete Exercise #9: Getting the Job Done Right before
moving on to the next section.

****

If you could make all these things happen by trying harder or working more hours or bribing/threatening trades (*Satisfaction by Luck*) then you wouldn't need this book. So it's time to get honest about why you're not hitting these goals, no matter how hard you try. What *specifically* is happening to block the success of projects?

In the next section, **Taking Inventory,** we examine our business practices. First, we identify *what* goes wrong on projects and *why* jobs are veering off-course. Next, we identify procedures and processes that are absent or ill functioning. Finally, we produce specific systems and procedures to circumvent or eliminate these project difficulties.

You may be thinking, "Who has time for analysis? I'm putting in 12-hour days as it is, working weekends, evenings and barely meeting deadlines now." I guarantee that if you don't have time to work *on* your business, you will spend plenty of time – later – fixing the problems.

If you don't have time to work *on* your business, you will spend plenty of time – later – fixing the problems.

Section 2: Taking Inventory

Identifying and improving business practices
A successful business regularly takes inventory.

 Thorough stocktaking helps the design business owner to identify which systems and procedures are working and where improvement is required. It is simply a fact-finding mission. It's not about "blame."

We will take inventory in five steps, A-E. The first step, A (**Getting the Job Done Right**), you should have completed in the previous section.

A.   Define **Getting the Job Done Right**.

B.   Identify what is *actually* happening with projects.

C.   Determine *why* problems occur, thus blocking ideals in **Getting the Job Done Right**.

D.   Determine what changes would eliminate these recurring problems.

E.   Create systems to produce required changes; thus circumventing problems.

A: **Getting the Job Done Right**.

- Beside "A" write only one of your targets/goals.

| What's actually happening? | → | Why is it happening? | → | What would eliminate problem? | → | Procedure required |

B: **What's actually happening?**

- Here we identify what is *actually* happening on projects (as it relates to the target/ goal listed in A), rather than what we "wish" were happening.

- Consider multiple projects and clients as you identify the behaviours, situations and actions you've encountered, especially if they repeat. Be thorough and list as many examples as possible. Focus initially on Column B only.

C: ***Why* is it happening? What's causing the reaction?**

- Determine *why* the situations in Column B are happening. Identify where projects are veering off course. The more honest you can be, the more helpful this exercise. It may be some consolation to know that identifying the *why* leads directly to a solution.

- In some cases, it will be obvious why the problems are arising. Perhaps you have a habit of showing up late to meetings or you frequently promise more than you can deliver. In other cases, you may have to speculate as to why the problem is occurring.

- Determine what you are doing (or not doing) that provokes each problem to occur. Identify any plausible reason for it. Put yourself in the client's shoes and ask yourself what would cause you to react in a similar manner. Remember, we are not concerned with "blame," we are merely identifying facts.

D.   What would eliminate the problem?

- Here we determine what would eliminate the problem. Where there is a "problem," there is likely a "solution." That's what we are looking for in this column.

- Identify any action you might take which would eliminate the difficulty noted in Column C.

- Identify any action or behaviour you should *not* take in future to eliminate the difficulty noted in Column C.

E: What actions/systems/procedures are required?

- Here we determine what that new practice, procedure or system looks like. What is its aim? How can it be broken down into systematic steps?

- Devise the procedure or system.

> **The examples provided on the following pages will guide you through the process.** Following the examples you will find a blank chart for your personal use.

SAMPLE EXERCISE: Taking Inventory

A. Getting the Job Done Right:

Example: Client is pleased with service and progress throughout the project.

B. What's Actually Happening?	C. Why is it Happening?	D. What would eliminate the problem?	E. Procedure or System Required

SAMPLE EXERCISE: Taking Inventory

A. Getting the Job Done Right:

Example: Client is pleased with service and progress throughout the project.

B. WHAT'S ACTUALLY HAPPENING?	C. WHY IS IT HAPPENING?	D. WHAT WOULD ELIMINATE THE PROBLEM?	E. PROCEDURE OR SYSTEM REQUIRED
Client gets too involved in project details; fussing about every thing that happens			
Client calls frequently with questions			
Client complains about job site conditions			
Client dislikes one of the trades			

SAMPLE EXERCISE: Taking Inventory

A. Getting the Job Done Right:

Example: Client is pleased with service and progress throughout the project.

B. WHAT'S ACTUALLY HAPPENING?	C. WHY IS IT HAPPENING?	D. WHAT WOULD ELIMINATE THE PROBLEM?	E. PROCEDURE OR SYSTEM REQUIRED
Client gets too involved in project details; fussing about everything that happens	1. Trades talk to client about issues on site or with job 2. Client is anxious about progress 3. Client is anxious about money 4. Client feels unacknowledged		
Client calls frequently with questions	1. Client isn't clear on next steps 2. We are not communicating next steps well enough		
Client complains about job site conditions	1. Job site is messy 2. Trades obviously don't know our on-site requirements		
Client dislikes one of the trades	1. This trade is difficult 2. He is causing job site tension 3. I have no one to replace him		

SAMPLE EXERCISE: Taking Inventory

A. Getting the Job Done Right:

Example: Client is pleased with service and progress throughout the project.

B. WHAT'S ACTUALLY HAPPENING?	C. WHY IS IT HAPPENING?	D. WHAT WOULD ELIMINATE THE PROBLEM?	E. PROCEDURE OR SYSTEM REQUIRED
Client gets too involved in project details; fussing about every thing that happens	1. Trades talk to client about issues on site or with job 2. Client is anxious about progress 3. Client is anxious about money 4. Client feels unacknowledged	1. Teach trades my rules 2. Advise client of next steps 3. Advise client of financial status 4. Acknowledge client concerns	
Client calls frequently with questions	1. Client isn't clear on next steps 2. We are not communicating next steps well enough	1. Advise client of next steps 2. Advise client of next steps	
Client complains about job site conditions	1. Job site is messy 2. Trades obviously don't know our on-site requirements	1. Teach trades rules 2. Teach trades rules	
Client dislikes one of the trades	1. This trade is difficult 2. He is causing job site tension 3. I have no one to replace him	1. Teach trades rules 2. Replace this trade with "A" Team – ask for recommendation	

Looking closely at Column D, we consider solutions to the specific issues, which were identified in Columns B and C. Our aim is to prevent these specific actions or behaviours from occurring in future. We do this by creating systems or procedures, which circumvent or eliminate the problems. We identify these systems and procedures in Column E. To illustrate, I've added suggestions to column E below:

SAMPLE EXERCISE: Taking Inventory

A. Getting the Job Done Right:

Example: Client is pleased with service and progress throughout the project.

B. WHAT'S ACTUALLY HAPPENING?	C. WHY IS IT HAPPENING?	D. WHAT WOULD ELIMINATE THE PROBLEM?	E. PROCEDURE OR SYSTEM REQUIRED
Client gets too involved in project details; fussing about every thing that happens	1. Trades talk to client about issues on site or with job	1. Teach trades my rules	1. Develop rules for working with KSDG. **
	2. Client is anxious about progress	2. Advise client of next steps	2. Apprise client of next steps with weekly meetings.
	3. Client is anxious about money	3. Advise client of financial status	3. Review financial status with monthly updates.
	4. Client feels unacknowledged	4. Acknowledge client concerns	4. Listen to concerns. Do not "defend." Following conversation, send email to outline nature of concern and action required.

** **Resource Guide to Excellence (RGE)** reviewed in next section.

Here's a second example which features a different issue in Column A, and suggestions for B, C, D, and E.

SAMPLE EXERCISE: Taking Inventory

A. Getting the Job Done Right:

Example: Client is pleased with service and progress throughout the project.

B. WHAT'S ACTUALLY HAPPENING?	C. WHY IS IT HAPPENING?	D. WHAT WOULD ELIMINATE THE PROBLEM?	E. PROCEDURE OR SYSTEM REQUIRED
Client complains about job site conditions	1. Job site is messy	1. Regular cleaning required. Define regular cleaning for trades and discuss rules with client in advance and ongoing.	1. Develop job site rules for trades. **
	2. Trades obviously don't know what we require	2. Teach trades rules	2. Develop job site rules for trades. **

** **Resource Guide to Excellence (RGE)** reviewed in next section.

Here's a third example, which features a different issue in column A, and suggestions for B, C, D, and E.

SAMPLE EXERCISE: Taking Inventory

A. Getting the Job Done Right:

Example: Client is pleased with service and progress throughout the project.

B. WHAT'S ACTUALLY HAPPENING?	C. WHY IS IT HAPPENING?	D. WHAT WOULD ELIMINATE THE PROBLEM?	E. PROCEDURE OR SYSTEM REQUIRED
Client is not sending any referrals our way	1. We are not asking for referrals	1. Ask for referrals	1. Create project evaluation and questionnaire – ask for referral. **
	2. Client is angry about timeline, budget, other, so won't refer	2. Eliminate issues and concerns regarding timeline, budget, etc.	2. Develop system to track timelines and budget. **
	3. Client is happy but still won't refer	3. Ask why the client won't refer	3. Follow up on any questionnaire with no referral.

Samples in **Kimberley Seldon's Business of Design™: Part 2.**

** Samples in **Kimberley Seldon's Business of Design™: Part 2.**

Now, it's your turn.

Since you've reviewed the samples provided, it's time to begin your own business inventory process. Take as many hours as you need to complete a thorough inventory. The only way to do this "wrong" is not to do it at all.

When you are finished **Taking Inventory** the systems and procedures you create will find a home in your **Operations Manual**.

 I guarantee you will be amazed at the insights gained from this work if you turn your full attention to the task, so don't delay.

On the following page you will find a blank chart for your use.

****

Complete **Exercises #10: Taking Inventory** before moving on to the next section.

****

EXERCISE #10: Taking Inventory

A. Getting the Job Done Right:

B. WHAT'S ACTUALLY HAPPENING?	C. WHY IS IT HAPPENING?	D. WHAT WOULD ELIMINATE THE PROBLEM?	E. PROCEDURE OR SYSTEM REQUIRED

This exercise is available for download at www.businessofdesign.com/worksheets.

123

Section 3: Growing the Operations Manual

In the previous sample exercises we identified a need for specific procedures or systems, which we listed in Column E (see example below).

SAMPLE EXERCISE: Taking Inventory

A. Getting the Job Done Right:

Example: Client is pleased with service and progress throughout the project.

B. WHAT'S ACTUALLY HAPPENING	C. WHY IS IT HAPPENING	D. WHAT WOULD ELIMINATE THE PROBLEM	E. PROCEDURE OR SYSTEM REQUIRED
Client gets too involved in project details; fussing about every thing that happens	1. Trades talk to client about issues on site or with job	1. Teach trades my rules	1. Develop rules for working with KSDG. **
	2. Client is anxious about progress	2. Advise client of next steps	2. Apprise client of next steps with weekly meetings.
	3. Client is anxious about money	3. Advise client of financial status	3. Review financial status monthly.
	4. Client feels unacknowledged	4. Acknowledge client concerns	4. Listen to concerns. Do not "defend."

Looking only at Column E, our task is to create or build the systems and procedures we've identified a need for. It's a painstaking process in some cases, but I've learned from first-hand experience that these procedures can change your business, and more importantly your life.

E. PROCEDURE OR SYSTEM REQUIRED	F. BUILD THE SYSTEM
1. Develop rules for working with KSDG.	1. The rules or **Resource Guide to Excellence** are reviewed in **Section 5** of this Chapter.
2. Apprise client of next steps with weekly meetings.	2. Create weekly staff meetings to review status of each project. At meeting, determine next steps for each client. Phone or email client (as preferred) with update from weekly meeting.
3. Review financial status monthly.	3. Create financial statement and send to each client along with monthly billable hours invoice. Ask client to acknowledge receipt of statement. Provide set office hours where the client can phone regarding financial statement or any other concern.
4. Listen to concerns. Do not "defend."	4. Listen to concerns. Do not "defend." Following conversation, send email which outlines nature of concern and agreed to action. Verify that client agrees with the assessment in the email. Schedule a follow up meeting to review issue and determine if it has been resolved satisfactorily.

I provided examples of some of our systems in **Chapter 5**. You will no doubt come up with many others.

> Once completed, place the new systems in your **Operations Manual**. You've probably figured out by now that the **Operations Manual** is never "complete" as it's a lifelong journey to improving your business.

Some procedures are directed at staff. Others are directed toward trades, sub-trades and suppliers. These latter systems, we refer to as project rules or **Resource Guide to Excellence (RGE)** which will be discussed in **Section 5** of this Chapter.

Section 4: Building the "A" Team

Choosing resources to fulfill project goals

When a new project begins, it's the responsibility of the design professional to evaluate the resources required and hire appropriate companies and individuals. It helps to start with a mission statement.

For example:

Kimberley Seldon Design Group Mission Statement

At KSDG we strive to serve our valued and respected clientele through a system of **Satisfaction by Design**. We rely on experience, expertise and impeccable integrity to complete projects on time, on budget, with consistently pleasing results.

Each of your resources (people) has contact with your client and can impact your client's opinion of you. Gulp. Choose your team carefully.

The "A" Team

In our office we refer to the "A" Team. These are partners who have made an investment in our firm's reputation. They are companies and individuals who strive to hit our corporate promise and are likely working toward their own personal and corporate goals as well. Building your own "A" Team takes time and experience. Here are some guidelines for "A" Team membership.

An "A" Team member:

- Consistently demonstrates a commitment to excellence that matches yours.

- Brings new insight to projects.

- Doesn't just give you what you ask for, but offers alternatives that improve job quality and client satisfaction.

- Understands their client is you and your firm. Mr. Jones or Mrs. Smith may be *your* client, but the "A" Team must <u>think of you as the final authority</u>.

- Acknowledges a promise to your client (Mr. Jones or Mrs. Smith) is equivalent to a commitment to you.

Obviously, in order for trades to commit to a promise they must know *precisely* what is at stake. It's your job to provide a clear set of guidelines, which in our office is referred to as the project rules or **Resource Guide to Excellence (RGE)** which will be reviewed in the next section.

The "B" Team

So what about the "B" Team? We have excellent trades we consider "B" Team in our office. Typically, a "B" Team trade is lacking in one particular area. Perhaps this trade has excellent skills and standards, but has difficulty adhering to timelines. Or, requires frequent supervision due to late arrivals or frequent sick days. In this case, I meet with the trade and let him/her know why he/she is part of our "B" Team. I review the areas that require improvement to move up to the "A" Team. I review the perks associated with being part of the "A" Team, namely first right of refusal on projects, more prestigious jobs, etc.

I've had "B" Team members move up to the "A" Team once they realize we are committed to excellence in deed. I've also had "A" Team members move to the "B" Team.

Section 5: Resource Guide to Excellence (RGE)

In our **Resource Management Chapter** we have agreed thus far:

- Your professional and personal happiness is impacted by your capacity for "**Getting the Job Done Right.**" In order to fulfill on that promise, the goals must be precisely defined.

- **Taking Inventory** allows us to identify how projects veer off course. This insight is used to create procedures and systems for preventing problems in future.

- The **Operations Manual** organizes all corporate systems and procedures into one, easily accessible location.

- An "**A**" **Team** makes it possible to satisfy you (the client) and meet corporate goals. However, trades must know the ground rules.

Remember, your trades *want* to satisfy you. Neatly defined goals make it easier for everyone to meet expectations and ultimately, satisfy the customer. We call these rules **RGE (Resource Guide to Excellence)**.

Believe me, I used to try getting my trades to do what I needed them to do by asking nicely, pleading, threatening, and finally using charm. It was neither professional nor terribly effective.

Today, I engage in none of that behaviour, yet my job sites work much more efficiently.

Instead of gimmicks and reliance on *Satisfaction by Luck*, I provide my resources with concrete rules for **Getting the Job Done Right** according to my standards. Since my trades know what the expectations are, we are working together toward common goals. We now have a similar language of mutual respect and conflict resolution. I enjoy much stronger relationships with trades and have an extremely high rate for pleasing clients.

> By providing specific points of reference for my resources, I make it possible for them to please me, and ultimately my clients.

We have rules for working on job sites. For instance, we ask that trades remove their outdoor shoes and put on indoor shoes or work boots as required. Let's say Mrs. H does not want trades to wear outdoor shoes in her house but Mrs. J doesn't worry about it. If the rule is flexible, someone is bound to leave shoes on in the wrong house. So we've determined it's better to set one rule for all projects.

On the following page, I've given you a sample of our **RGE**. Over the years, I've consulted with many of our valued trades for input on developing this list.

Thank you to Michael Tafts, owner of G. Pederson and Associates Construction for his guidance on this section.

Kimberley Seldon
DESIGN GROUP

RESOURCE GUIDE TO EXCELLENCE

Kimberley Seldon Design Group Mission Statement

At **KSDG** we strive to serve our valued and respected clientele through a system of **Satisfaction by Design.** We rely on experience, expertise and impeccable integrity to complete projects on time, on budget, with consistently pleasing results.

Dear Valued Tradesperson,

A promise to **KSDG** is a commitment not to be undertaken lightly. It is our aim, with these rules, which we refer to as the **RESOURCE GUIDE TO EXCELLENCE** to create an atmosphere of harmony with each project. We are committed to your growth and well-being. We ask for reciprocal consideration. Together, we can produce consistently pleasing results for the customers who hire us.

General

- You are engaged to work for **KSDG** on behalf of our clients. Therefore, your client is **KSDG**, regardless of project location. All direction for work comes directly and only from **KSDG**.

- We expect our trades to think outside the box, add value to our projects and improve our ideas. Don't just give us what we asked for. Prompt us to greater knowledge. Teach us more about your business.

- All trades must provide proof of insurance and workman's compensation (where required). **KSDG** keeps this paperwork on file and requires updates annually.

- Under no circumstances is the trade allowed to accept any offer to work directly or indirectly with one of **KSDG's** clients; all interactions happen through **KSDG**. **KSDG** will not be responsible for any work done without our express authority.

- No meaningful, job-related conversations should take place with **KSDG's** clients unless **KSDG** is present. In the event a job-related conversation is unavoidable or does take place in the absence of **KSDG**, it is the trade's responsibility to inform **KSDG** of details of the conversation immediately.

- Any deviation from the schedule, budget or product must be approved through **KSDG**.

Job Site Behaviour

- Observe professional rules of conduct – dress code, behaviour on site.

- Never park in or block the client's driveway (don't even ask).

- No loud music on site.

- No swearing on site.

- Work boots and hardhat required during any renovation. If you have subcontracts or employees on site, it is your responsibility to ensure they follow the rules as well.

- Outside shoes must be removed and clean shoes or work boots (as required) worn on job sites.

- Job site condition is important to everyone. At end of day, **KSDG** expects the job site to be broom swept, and cleared of any obstructions, which might cause an accident. A neat job site sends a message of "orderliness" to our clients.

Producing a Successful Bid

- **KSDG** expects a written quote returned to us within 72 hours of on-site review (Trade Day) of proposed job, where a single service such as painting, floor finishing, or closet organizing is required. For trades requiring a full drawing package, we expect a written quote returned to us within two weeks from receipt of full drawing package.

- When you receive a full drawing package from **KSDG** for purposes of estimating, we respectfully request you review the package within 24 hours to determine if there is further information required. If we do not hear from you, we assume you have everything you need to get firm, written prices to us by the agreed-upon time period.

- Our resources are required to produce a written commitment to start date, time line and completion date at the outset of each project.

- We expect our resources to provide **KSDG** with reasonable fees for all work performed.

Failure to comply with the RGE may result in:

a. Financial penalties such as holding back funds.

b. Immediate stoppage of work and dismissal from project.

c. No further work provided from **KSDG**.

Thank you for your attention and adherence to these rules.
Please let us know how we can serve you better.

In my experience, skilled trades prefer working with professional design firms. We provide structure and discipline in an industry that often lacks these qualities. Trades tell me that it is much easier to work with a design firm than with individual clients since the designer manages bookkeeping, billing, collections, client meetings, and so on.

If one of your trades balks at compliance with these rules, you know right away you have a problem. Trust me when I say you cannot afford to work with anyone who doesn't adopt your policy of reliance on experience, expertise and impeccable integrity to complete projects on time, on budget, with consistently pleasing results.

Remember, the expectations captured in your **RGE** do not deviate with individual clients. These are standardized benchmarks that must be met each and every time.

Ask your trades what they think about the experience of working with you.

Have you made their "A" Team?

Section 6: Better Trade Relations

Better trade relations = Better business

I do not want to leave anyone with the impression that trades are the "bad guys" and you have to watch out for them. In fact, quite the opposite is true. **I can't count the number of times a contractor or tradesperson has improved a project, or saved us from making a mistake.**

 Your resources – trades, sub-trades, contractors, suppliers and manufacturers – are ideally situated to provide guidance on improving your business. They can offer suggestions for improving jobsite quality, service and performance.

Ask your trades what they think about the experience of working with you.

Valued trades keep you apprised of situations that develop when you are not on site. They are your "eyes and ears." I've had trades call me when an issue threatens to develop, such as the time a tradesperson warned me about an employee's questionable work. That phone call saved me endless trouble. Clients sometimes "let down their hair" around trades. Providing that information is passed onto you, invaluable insight is gained and a future incident may be avoided.

With professional trades on your team, you don't have to know everything. If you spend time and ask questions, your suppliers can teach you so much. Early on in my career I thought I had to know everything. That made me afraid to ask the "dumb" questions. Today, I realize I can't know everything, but that a trade specializing in a particular area does.

Finally, make sure you express satisfaction and gratitude often. Tradespeople most often join a project after it's started and frequently finish before full completion. It's rare they are invited back to receive praise from your client. Let them know that they are instrumental in any success. In my experience, they appreciate that more than you can imagine.

Money, money, money, money, money. There, I've said it. It's not so hard, really.

In **Chapter Eight** we commit ourselves to clarity: *What* to charge, *How* to charge, and *When* to collect. If you manage these tasks your money "problems" will disappear. You'll be happier and your clients will be too.

Plus, how to eliminate your **Cash Flow** problems.

And, what **9 Money Managers** (aka clients) taught me about invoicing.

Charging for Services

In this Chapter

- Section 1: Determining Hourly Fees
- Section 2: Tracking Hours
- Section 3: Invoicing and Collecting Billable Hours
- Section 4: Managing Discounts
- Section 5: Markup/Overhead
- Section 6: Collections and Cash Flow

Total Transparency

Total transparency? You're probably wondering if I've lost my mind. You're likely thinking: "I can't afford to operate with total transparency. I'm barely making ends meet now."

> Every difficulty you encounter with regards to money stems from a lack of communication. If you are clear about what you charge, how you charge, and when it's due, the majority of your money "problems" will disappear. You'll be happier and your clients will be too.

The exchange of money for services carries with it an obligation. You cannot provide outstanding service unless you are operating a mature business, which practices sound business principals. Professional businesses charge for their services and in most cases, the fees are easy to identify. Requiring clients to "figure out" how you charge isn't acceptable.

You can't afford *not* to be 100% transparent when it comes to money.

> Would you hire a lawyer who hemmed and hawed about fees, eat in a restaurant that didn't post prices, or shop in a shoe store where the sales clerk made up the price to suit his mood?

If you are squirming or unsure when asked about your fees, it sends a message you are "making it up as you go along," or worse, that you are trying to "get away with something."

For most "creative" business owners, that isn't the case. Perhaps you've never had an opportunity to compare your fees to others. Maybe you are uncomfortable speaking about money, or you think it's rude to focus on such a crass topic.

 I've met designers who insist they "love what they do, it isn't about the money" and yet, when pressed they are Bitter, Angry, Disappointed and Resentful about their salary for a vocation they profess to love.

Let's talk money!

Section 1: Determining Hourly Fees

An era has come and gone and maybe you didn't even realize it. In the infancy of design and décor, decorators like Dorothy Draper or Elsie de Wolfe charged exorbitant fees for their services. This thing called *design* seemed like magic, and provided a new kind of "status" the well-heeled were eager to embrace. Consequently, design fees could be justified by the fact that *what* these early decorators did was a total mystery to the homeowners who hired them.

Sources were top secret, with names jealously guarded in address books. And since no customer could price shop, these early designers were able to name their fee.

Today, however, there is nothing secret about our business, what with shelter magazines revealing insider tips, TV shows turning the whole process into entertainment, and the Internet telling it all.

That was then. This is now.

Since there is no mystery left, let's agree that *transparency* is the only option. Transparency makes it easier for clients to trust your integrity. And, in my opinion you cannot run a Mature business without integrity.

I hear frequent objections to this opinion when I teach **Kimberley Seldon's Business of Design**™. Most say:

> "Sure, I bill the client for *some* hours, but not *all* of them. They would never pay if I billed them for everything. But that's ok, because I make up for it in other ways."

Huh? What other ways?!?

Here are a few gems I've personally run up against on projects:

- The former designer (we came in mid-way through the project) provided the client with a sample from a high-end fabric house (Beacon Hill), and then substituted a "knock off" from a fabric jobber. When I needed more fabric, we discovered the switch.

- A tradesperson offered to give my contractor "a little something extra" at the end of the project, if he let some shoddy workmanship slide on one of our projects.

- A contractor (which was hired directly by the client) purchased supplies for two projects and placed them onto a single bill. When it was presented to the client the inconsistency was discovered. (The contractor was fired.)

> **Call it what you will, but these under-the-table
> games have a name -- FRAUD.**

I cannot tell you how many "cheating" stories clients have shared with me regarding previous projects they've attempted. This means that before I've even done the consultation, the client is suspicious. In my experience:

The best way to gain a client's trust is with impeccable integrity and a system of transparent practices.

Unless your contract specifies randomly putting in a little "extra" here and there, you cannot operate in this manner and maintain your integrity. Do not, even for one minute, try to justify this errant behaviour. It hurts the whole industry.

That's the old way of doing business; these days it doesn't wash. The reality is, our industry has matured and it is each firm's duty to grow with it. By clinging to some old – and shady – practices, clients suspect us of having less than honorable standards. Only legitimate methods of service and *reasonable compensation* will do.

Reasonable compensation. What's that?

How about this definition:

Getting paid for the *actual* hours you contribute towards the completion of a job on behalf of a client; where payment is consistent with your experience, responsibility and liability.

> Too often I meet design professionals who do not bill the client for *all* of their hours. Fine, if you don't mind working for free. However, **they do mind -- very much**.

It starts with the best of intentions and the reasoning goes something like this:

- "Well, that didn't take long, and Mrs. Smith is so nice. I won't bill her for this."

OR

- "That took a long time, Mrs. Smith will not be happy. I guess I won't bill her for all of this. Even though I accomplished a huge amount of work in thirty minutes yesterday. I hope Mrs. Smith knows how lucky she is." (grumble, grumble)

OR

- "Mrs. Smith is going to freak when she sees my bill. I can't deal with that now. I'll just eat it this month and make up for it next month."

As the project rolls along, a number of these justifications occur. Mrs. Smith gets used to being charged for some things and not others. It seems a little arbitrary, but that's ok. How does Mrs. Smith know you didn't bill her for all your hours? You told her. After all, you want some credit for being such a fabulous person, right?

When the next invoice rolls around Mrs. Smith questions the number of hours and can't understand why she was billed for a task that seems like another she wasn't billed for in the past. You follow her logic and agree it's a good idea for you to knock those hours off your invoice too. Over several months, you begin to stew about the number of hours you've worked for free. Soon, you start to be annoyed with Mrs. Smith. Why? She didn't go into the project assuming you wouldn't charge for your time.

Can you see once again this is a situation of your own creation? You have literally taught Mrs. Smith that your time is not valuable, that you deserve to be paid for only *some* of your expertise (hours), and that your fees are so extravagant you can afford to give away hours for free.

Regardless, *it is not the client's fault.*

 It won't be long until you find yourself in the company of those old friends Bitter, Angry, Disappointed and Resentful.

It's essential for all of us to educate our clients and make improvements as an industry.

The reality is:

- Some tasks happen quickly, others take more time.

- Some tasks are pleasant, some less so.

- Some tasks seem valid to a client, in other cases, you may have to explain to the customer why it was necessary for you to perform the work in the manner you chose.

Remember, **clients *want* you to succeed**. Clients do not hire design professionals only to hope in secret they will fail. In my experience when I provide a client with a legitimate position, they nearly always enthusiastically support it. Why? Because it allows me to accomplish agreed upon goals that benefit the project.

Naturally, you want to charge an hourly fee that is consistent with your experience, responsibility and liability. In other words, charge what you are worth. Hmmmm, so what exactly are you worth?

EXERCISE #11: What is your Current Rate for Billing?

How do you charge customers for your services? Define every method you have for charging the client. Consider hourly fees and any other means of compensation such as mark up on product or services. Be specific.

1. _____
2. _____
3. _____
4. _____
5. _____
6. _____

Consider money practices which worry you or make you feel uncomfortable. Are you "protecting" clients from knowing all the ways you charge? Describe any instances where charging for services feels unclear or poorly defined.

1. _____
2. _____
3. _____
4. _____
5. _____
6. _____

This exercise is available for download at www.businessofdesign.com/worksheets.

****

Complete **Exercises #11: What is your Current Rate for Billing?**
before moving on to the next section.

****

It you are like the vast majority of working professionals who have attended my courses, you are not charging enough. Not only that, I'm shocked at the number of working professionals who have "flexible" fees or charge different amounts for different clients.

I'm asking you to consider what your value is and weigh that against your liability. Consider if you will these "average" salaries taken from businesses that are local to me in the city of Toronto, Ontario:

- Nails $ 25 / 30 min (average) = $ 50/hour
- IT Service Provider $ 90 / hour = $ 90/hour
- Haircut $ 70 / 45 min (average) = $ 92 /hour
- Bikini Wax $ 30 / 15 min (average) = $120/hour

Is it safe to say that none of these professionals has more responsibility or liability than you do, as the owner of a design firm? If that's true, then why are your rates lower than those for an IT provider or the person who cuts your hair? **Perhaps it's time for a raise.**

**Now why would I teach you this when you'll be my *competition?*

There is enough work for everyone. What I want to see is an **industry of peers**, with a great divide between "dabblers" and pros. If you are an interior designer living in an urban center and charging $75 per hour, not only do you devalue the industry, but you position yourself as a dabbler. It's also likely that at that hourly rate, you are playing fast and loose with charging for services and product and "getting away with" a little extra here and there.

I'm advocating instead that you charge a legitimate fee and bill for only the hours that you work.

Adjust rate for location and experience

At the same time, you may have to adjust your hourly rate based on location. Those living in rural areas typically have a lower rate (though not always). You will also want to consider your level of expertise. If you are new to the business, you will charge a lower rate. But should it be lower than the fee for a mani-pedi?

 Consider this too – customers perceive value based on nothing more than *rate of compensation*.

Let me give you an example.

Let's say you're at a cocktail party and you meet two lawyers. Since you need to hire an attorney you ask Lawyer #1 what she charges. She stutters and stammers and finally gives you an hourly fee in the neighborhood of $150 per hour. It takes her several minutes to spit this out because she's busy justifying her degree and the cost of doing business. She quickly adds that you seem lovely however, so she's probably willing to negotiate a lower rate to make it work for you.

Moving on to Lawyer #2, you ask the same question, "What do you charge for your services?" Lawyer #2 looks you straight in the eye and says $450 per hour and I'm worth every penny.

If you really need a lawyer, which one will you hire? Isn't it true that the lack of confidence and degree of "flexibility" demonstrated by Lawyer #1 has you questioning her expertise from the start?

In my experience teaching **Kimberley Seldon's Business of Design**™ the majority of business owners I meet sound like Lawyer #1.

It's far better to determine an **hourly fee** (based on location and expertise) and state that fee in the most *straightforward* manner possible.

Since I've already mentioned lawyers, let's look at the fee structure for a law firm.

The lawyer provides a service that, like ours, is less mysterious with each passing year. Nonetheless, it's a legitimate and warranted profession. People are willing to pay for a lawyer when they need one. Lawyers charge for their expertise by the hour, like we do. Law firms commonly charge different rates depending on experience. Junior lawyers, for example, charge less and take on tasks more senior partners might find monotonous. Senior lawyers bill at a higher rate because of their experience. **The design professional is wise to adopt the same model. It works and your clients are likely familiar with its basic principals.**

If you had an important job for a lawyer, would you really refuse to pay more for someone whose expertise was greater? Or, would you insist that the senior lawyer prepare every element of your case, even if a junior could take on some of the work with no ill effect?

Clients are perfectly reasonable people.

Speak to them in a *straightforward* manner about fees and billing practices. These details must be clearly and precisely defined in your **contract**.

(**Contracts** are reviewed in **Kimberley Seldon's Business of Design™: Part 2.**)

Is it time to give yourself a raise?
If you follow the directions and grow your business as outlined in this workbook the answer is **Yes!** If you are operating a mature business and practicing **Satisfaction by Design** the answer is **Yes!**

Be aware – the higher your hourly fee, the greater the expectation for performance. The client will and *should* expect you to live up to that fee.

In my office, like a law firm, we have a sliding scale of fees based on experience. In 2009, **Kimberley Seldon Design Group** billed our clients as follows:

Principal_____$325 per hour   Junior _____$115 per hour

Senior_____$195 per hour   Intermediate _____$145 per hour

Administration_____$ 75 per hour

Now it's your turn:

- What's your current hourly rate? _____

- What do you think your hourly rate should be? _____

- What is your new hourly rate? _____

There, doesn't that feel better?

Once you've established a reasonable hourly fee, the next challenge is keeping track of those hours.

Section 2: Tracking Hours

In the previous section I suggest - every difficulty you experience with regards to money stems from lack of communication. Not only is this true when it comes to charging for your hours, it's equally true when it comes to accounting for those hours.

Tracking your hours is a daily obligation and should not be taken lightly. I teach my staff to write a **thorough description** of each and every task.

 The best way to log hours is to imagine the client watching over your shoulder. If the client sees the validity of the work and understands the effort put into it, they will not object to paying for the time it takes to accomplish the task.

Let's say you meticulously log hours and present an invoice at the end of the month as promised. Mr. H says, "What? There's no way billable hours add up to $5,000 this month. Show me where those hours went." Do not be angry with Mr. H. He has every right to ask how his money is being spent. You would ask if the situation were reversed.

In this scenario, how does the *mature* design business owner respond?

a. Are you kidding me? How dare you question my integrity?

b. Well, we really did a lot of work for you Mr. H. But if you're not happy, let's just forget about this month's invoice. I'm having a grand time working for you and my staff won't mind waiting a couple of weeks for their paychecks.

c. Let me send you the log sheets today. Once you've had a chance to review them, let's have a conversation and see if you have any questions.

Sounds like a fantasy scenario, but years ago, when I was in that situation, I would immediately get nervous. I was so busy working and would think: "I don't have time to deal with this now." But it could not be avoided, so I'd phone the client and outline the work performed. Then I would somewhat grudgingly offer to prepare a log sheet analysis so the client could review it.

Keep in mind; we already had the log sheets, filled in by each staff member. However, we had to cut and paste each person's hours into a single document. This process might take an hour or more to complete. That wasn't the tough part. The difficulty was finding *time* in an already over-burdened day to get them done. So, it might take a few days for me to get back to the client with the log sheets.

> Given the time to procure the **log sheets,** no wonder Mr. H was *considering the possibility* I was busy "making them up." **That wasn't the truth, but it was the *perception.***

Thanks to the process of **Taking Inventory (Chapter 7, Section 2),** I was able to define the *problem:* a perception of deception when it came to log sheets. And identify the *solution:* produce log sheets within 24 hours. I also created a procedure that identified our log sheet policy and outlined a more efficient way to track hours and provide log sheets within a 24-hour period.

Guess what?

The new time frame changed everything.

Once I was able to provide detailed time sheets within hours, it eliminated the perception of dishonesty. That diffused more than half the problem. From there, I was able to talk with clients in a respectful manner and address concerns in an honest, open fashion. I listened without "defending."

On the rare occasions when a client identified a task that seemed unwarranted, I removed the time from the invoice. Then, I reviewed the situation with staff, explaining the client's point of view without blame. I learned something from these experiences and so did my staff. These conversations often made us more efficient at our jobs.

In some cases, the description for the task was weak, making it difficult for the client to justify the work. In other cases, a task appeared more than once on a log sheet without explanation as to why. (Let's face it, there are times when despite your best efforts, you cannot solve an issue with one phone call.)

In nearly every instance, the client was able to see the effort and justify the time allotted. The process of reviewing the log sheets provided the client with insight into the complexity of our work and it reminded me of our responsibility to use the client's money with care.

> Today, I expect my clients to hold me to the *highest standards*. I demand that from myself and from everyone who works with me.

Next, you will find another page from my own **Operations Manual**. This one outlines how we categorize and log hours on behalf of clients.

SECTION 5: Interior Design	POLICY #: 45678
TOPIC: Logging Billable Hours	
BY: Erin Mercer	PAGE: 1 of 3
AUTHORIZATION SIGNATURE	

KSDG invoices its customers by calculating hours spent on specific tasks. We are not billing for our time, we are billing for expertise. We quantify our expertise in increments of time, which we calculate as follows:

.25 = 15 minutes
.50 = 30 minutes
.75 = 45 minutes
1.0 = 1 hour

Coding Tasks

To categorize the work provided on behalf of a client, we use various codes, which we assign to each task. Our codes include:

M	Meetings	client meetings; face to face
PM	Phone Meeting	client phone calls; voice to voice
PD	Planning & Design	project review, drawing, internal team meetings, creative concept work, execution of required tasks
S	Sourcing	sourcing product; including on-line resourcing
A	Administration	administrative tasks; duties not requiring designer supervision
I	Installation	time spent on a job site, with client not present (where client is present, label M)
TD	Trade Day	initial, on site meeting to capture measurements, review inventory and confirm client's direction for work
NC	No Charge	an error made by KSDG (not its manufacturers or suppliers) must be corrected at no charge.

Billable hours must be:

- **Precise.** Be meticulous when tracking hours.

- **Logged daily.** Failure to do so increases risk of inaccuracy and may result in termination.

- **Written in straightforward and descriptive language.** Imagine the client is standing over your shoulder reading your hours. Make sure your actions are warranted and necessary, and then write them down in clear detail.

- **Sorted at the end of the month.** Then, reviewed by the Principal (or Finance Administrator) for invoicing purposes.

Client requests review of billable hours

KSDG has a commitment to produce details of a monthly invoice for billable hours within 24 hours (assuming business day) in response to a client request. For that reason, each designer must maintain hours daily. If a client requests copies of billable hours for any month, notify the Finance Administrator immediately. The Finance Administrator or Principal will contact the client directly to review the log sheets and invoicing.

Logging Tasks

Each task is logged by date, client last name, description and code. When describing work performed, be precise and use "action" words. For example: scheduled, confirmed, inspected, reviewed, revised, sourced, etc.

If a group of tasks takes place on behalf of a single client, and carries the same code (as shown below), then it's possible to group the tasks within a single time frame. For example:

Date	Client	Description	Code	Time
02/07/10	Jones	Phoned client to request meeting date, confirmed meeting time with three trades, reviewed agenda and packed trade day bag.	PD	0.50

Because each of these tasks falls under the umbrella of Planning and Design (PD) they can be grouped together.

If tasks fall into different categories, they must be logged independently for accurate tracking.

Other Logging Tips

- If you are off-site all day it's important that your hours get logged. You can: phone someone at the office to log your hours for you; phone your own voicemail and detail your hours; or send yourself an email or text.

- Some designers find it helpful to update hours at the end of each day and project tasks for the next day. In other words, you can write the next days "to do" list on your log sheet the night before. Then, as the tasks are completed the next day, you can add the time required to complete the task to the log sheet.

- If you attend a meeting or work directly with another team member you must identify that person on the description line for the task. For example, if you attend a client meeting with a coworker (Erin Mercer) then beside your description for the event add (EM).

- Record events and corporate charity work under the project name, e.g. Habitat for Humanity, Gilda's Club, Junior League Show House.

We never promise projects will be mistake-free.

That's impossible because human error is a reality.

Billing for "Mistakes"

Should you bill for mistakes? Yes and No.

If you or one of your staff makes a mistake (for example, transposes a number on an order resulting in the wrong item being ordered) then we do not bill for the time it takes to correct that error. However, if one of your resources made the mistake – a trade, sub-trade, manufacturer or supplier – then we do bill for the time to fix the error.

What? But that's not fair; it's not the client's fault this mistake happened, why should they be billed?

1. If the client were working without a design professional, they would spend their time getting the situation corrected.

2. Can you imagine a law firm that didn't bill for time to regroup and create a new strategy when one avenue proved fruitless?

The work we do is not linear. It is fraught with subtle twists and turns. As *experts*, we navigate those curves much more efficiently than a non-professional.

We never promise projects will be mistake-free. That's impossible because human error is a reality. On a small project there might be 50 different people or companies you deal with and, on a large project, that number grows exponentially. (At the end of the book you will find an article that I wrote for Style at Home that provides more insight on this topic).

Even with great systems in place, it's not possible for the designer to catch every error before it's made. We do prevent myriad errors from happening through careful preparation and on site review. In most cases, the client is blissfully unaware of these challenges and potential missteps or catastrophes.

Clients are smart people, and most have some experience with trying to get companies to make repairs or show up for an appointment and the frustration that can result. If the client were doing the work without you, chances are they would not get the satisfaction (resolution) that you get, by virtue of your relationship with trades and the fact that you are a repeat customer. This is especially true for companies working on a one-time-only basis, where they are less concerned with completing deficiencies or punch list items than a company that works repeatedly for a designer.

Example from KSDG case file.

A client once asked to see our log sheets. After reviewing, she questioned an item on a junior designer's log sheet. It concerned an incorrect fabric arriving from a supplier. On the log sheets, my junior staff member logged thirty minutes at her rate of $115 per hour to:

- Open the bolt and determine it was the wrong fabric by comparing our CFA (cutting for approval).

- Call the supplier to inform them of the issue and receive instructions for returning the fabric for replacement.

- Phone the upholsterer to let him know the anticipated fabric was delayed.

- Re-order the correct fabric.

- Determine a new delivery date for the order.

The client did not understand why she should have to pay for this time, as it wasn't her fault. I think that's a reasonable assumption for someone who hasn't been educated as to the process. I explained to the client what the alternative would be, if we hadn't checked when we received the fabric:

- The wrong fabric would have been sent directly to the upholsterer.

- The upholsterer would have committed the wrong fabric to the right sofa.

- The sofa would have been delivered to the client's house where it would have been met with surprise and unhappiness.

- The movers would have to be hired to pick up the wrong sofa and return it to the upholsterer's shop.

- The fabric would have to be reordered.

- The sofa reupholstered.

- And the movers would have to be hired again to deliver the correct sofa to the client.

By the way, guess who gets to pay for the extra delivery charges, new fabric and second upholstery job? That's right, *it's you*. Are you sure you are comfortable charging $75 per hour for your services? You may want to re-think that.

Take a look at the **Sample Log Sheet** on the next page.

Kimberley Seldon

DESIGN GROUP

Sample Log Sheet

Designer: _Kathy Seale_

Month: _February_

Date	Client	Description	Code	Time
2-02-10	Gilliam	Met with clients on site to review floor plans and elevations.	M	1.50
2-02-10	Abells	Reviewed revised drawings, noted required changes and submitted to junior for processing.	PD	0.75
2-02-10	Gilliam	Sourced fabrics for main floor and pool house.	S	3.00
2-02-10	Schafer	Met with client's contractor to review proposed skylight, built-ins and wood samples. Determined selections and next steps. (KJ)	I	2.75
2-02-10	Schafer	Followed up from meeting with emails and direction to: carpenter, cabinetry shop, contractor and client.	PD	0.25
2-03-10	Crocker	Spoke with client regarding site supervision schedule, next meeting and final sign off on drawings.	PM	0.50
2-04-10	Steen	Trade Day. Captured measurements for space planning, measured existing inventory, prepared furnishings schedule and confirmed job details with client. (BT, KJ)	TD	4.5

Log Sheet

Designer: _____ **Month:** _____

Date	Client	Description		Code	Time

This form is available for download at www.businessofdesign.com/worksheets.

Section 3: Invoicing and Collecting Billable Hours

Once you are tracking hours meticulously and effectively, the next hurdle is getting those hours translated into an invoice for your client. Again, industry practices vary widely in this regard. It is not uncommon for "creative" business owners to send invoices to clients at irregular intervals. This makes it difficult for your client to manage his/her money and to keep on top of payments with ease. Often, I hear designers say, "Money is not important, I focus on the job and invoicing is a nuisance."

Hmmm....

> # I maintain that money is *quite* important – particularly to your clients!

Invoicing may be a nuisance, but clients still need to know when to expect invoices and when they are due. And frankly, you need to *get paid*.

Invoice clients with regularity

Mature businesses typically have a firm commitment regarding timing of invoices. Some firms send them every two weeks, for others it's a weekly occurrence. In my office, we bill clients on a monthly basis. This allows the client an opportunity to assess financial viability at regular and consistent intervals. And in the event the client is uncomfortable with the amount being billed, the workload can be readjusted and new priorities determined.

We log hours for clients on a daily basis. At the end of each month, the Finance Administrator reviews the log sheets from all staff members. It is her job to translate those hours into invoices for each client. If the Finance Administrator has a question about tasks performed, she will ask the designer for clarification. Once the hours are sorted, reviewed and tallied, monthly invoices are produced and sent to the clients.

What's the big deal if you are late sending invoices? After all, the client won't mind because they won't have to pay for a while. For one thing, the client will get a false sense of project costs. Imagine the shock of receiving two or three months' fees all at once. Furthermore, by the time you allow fees to accumulate for several months, you are likely to get into a Cash Flow crunch. If that happens you may end up pestering the client about payment, thus creating a perception of deception.

It's far better to establish a firm time when the client can expect the invoice.

With that guideline in place, you will also want to clarify when payment of the invoice is due. Because our work is performed *before* the client is invoiced, it is our policy that invoices for design fees are due upon receipt, allowing a reasonable time for review.

If you allow a 30 or 60-day lag between receipt of invoice and payment of invoice you are likely to run into a **Cash Flow** problem, especially if you have more than one client (**Cash Flow** is reviewed in **Section 6**). Of course, these policies must also be clearly stated in your contract, which you will review in detail with any new client. (**Contracts** are reviewed in **Kimberley Seldon's Business of Design™: Part 2.**)

Remember, it's the client's right to review your log sheets, so either have them ready to send to the client should they ask or send them automatically with your invoice.

Collect invoices with regularity

Above I state our policy that invoices are due upon receipt, allowing a reasonable time for review.

What's a reasonable time for review?

Since all difficulties with money stem from a lack of communication, it's important to clearly state these expectations in your contract.

We ask our clients to review monthly invoices and make any inquiries **within five business days** of receipt of invoice. We provide log sheets in the event there are any questions regarding the number of hours and how they were calculated. Next, we schedule a meeting (by phone or in person at the client's convenience) to review the invoice and log sheets. Following this review, we ask that fees be paid in full.

> ## 99% of the time the fees are paid in full following this procedure.

For fees that remain outstanding after this review and/or up to thirty days, we provide the following contingency: **We halt work until all outstanding fees are paid in full.**

No exceptions. None.

Let me emphasize this — we halt work until *all outstanding fees are paid in full*.

Obviously, if a client has not paid his/her design fees for two months in a row, something is wrong. Perhaps they are experiencing a minor **Cash Flow** problem. Perhaps they are concerned with mounting design fees? Perhaps there is a bigger problem — and if so, you need to know that now, before you go any further.

> I've learned through teaching **Kimberley Seldon's Business of Design**™ that rules - even the very best rules - won't protect you if you don't follow them. Consistently!

EXERCISE #12: Rules for Invoicing and Collecting

Write down some of your own rules for Invoicing and Collecting – be as detailed as possible. Name as many as you can, both written and unwritten.

1. _____
2. _____
3. _____
4. _____
5. _____
6. _____
7. _____
8. _____

Consider practices that are not working for you; problems that occur with regularity. Can you think of a "rule" that might make this situation better? If so, write it here.

1. _____
2. _____
3. _____
4. _____
5. _____
6. _____
7. _____
8. _____

This exercise is available for download at www.businessofdesign.com/worksheets.

My clients love that we share our discount. I find this approach works brilliantly and you will too.

Section 4: Managing Discounts

As with billable hours, the key to managing designer trade discounts is transparency. The client expects to pay a reasonable fee for purchases. They are also aware of the general concept of designer discounts. **But, here's the thing about designer discounts:**

- They are not nearly as big as they used to be.

- They are nowhere near as large as your client imagines.

- They belong to you, a courtesy for being a repeat or volume customer.

There is no set standard for dealing with designer discounts. But here are some typical practices.

ONE

Some design firms keep any and all discounts obtained from suppliers, manufacturers and retailers, which means the client is paying retail for the cost of the item.

TWO

Some design firms charge a markup (a fee, over and above the actual cost of the item) on every item purchased. The markup can be anywhere from 15-50%. In this scenario, unless you are sourcing wholesale product exclusively, the client may pay more than retail for purchases. This approach works well for commercial projects where most purchases come from wholesale sources.

THREE

I prefer a third scenario, which was generously shared with me years ago by another designer named Lynn Raitt. Her suggestion was this – share any discounts with clients fifty-fifty. This actually saves the client money by allowing them to benefit from purchases at below retail prices. It also provides you, the designer, with incentive for getting deeper discounts on the client's behalf, because you benefit too. It's a win-win situation.

When I meet with new clients and explain this system, they immediately see how these savings can underwrite or offset some of our design fees. In other words, by paying less than retail for purchases, it renders some design hours free. That's right. Free.

I found that charging retail or charging a percentage above cost (systems I have tried in the past) actually encouraged the client to purchase the furniture through another avenue - one that would offer them the discount. The client might have a family member or friend who's a "designer". Or, a store might pass on the "designer's discount" to give further incentive to a customer (yes, I know they are not supposed to, but you cannot fault a company for trying to stay in business or remain competitive). With either of these scenarios, someone other than you purchases the product.

Here's what could go wrong:

The client will still expect you to be responsible for the item's delivery and its condition upon arrival. Therefore, you must be emphatically clear about all aspects of the item in question before the friend or family member orders it. Let's look at a typical purchase for a sofa.

Before placing an order for a sofa you may need to determine the following:

- Is it skirted or with legs? What shape are the legs; cabriole or straight, carved or fluted? Are the legs stained in French walnut or mahogany? Or, are the legs painted and if so, what colour and is it matte or gloss?

- If it's skirted, what style is the skirt? Waterfall? Pleated? Is there trim on the skirt? If so, is it bullion, braid, cord? Where is it placed? At the edge, along the top, does it continue around the sides?

- Is there piping and if so, is it self, double or contrast piping?

- What about cushions? Are they loose-back or tight-back or a modification based on your clients needs? Sandwich-down seat or all-down, or all-foam?

I think you get the picture.

Despite the fact that you did not "order" the item, you are likely to be held fully responsible for its arrival and good luck passing the blame onto the friend or family member who kindly offered to share their discount. In the end, is the client really saving money? Would they opt for this scenario if you made it clear you would accept no responsibility for the condition or timing of the item in question? I doubt it.

Section 5: Markup

Perhaps the most challenging aspect of charging for services involves the hiring and management of resources such as general contractor, subcontractors and tradespeople. While a standardized, *industry-wide* policy would alleviate a lot of guesswork it doesn't exist.

In my experience, industry professionals sometimes see this as an area where they can make up for not billing enough hours or charge "a little extra" to compensate for a loss elsewhere. After all, how will the client know what tradespeople are charging you? Honestly, I can think of hundreds of ways this information can come to light. So why place your reputation in jeopardy?

 Make this part of a *transparent system* of **Satisfaction by Design**.

The suggestions I provide for you in this book and in my course, **Kimberley Seldon's Business of Design**™ work for me. However, when formulating your billing and invoicing practices I recommend you seek legal and accounting advice to ensure you are working within the law and in your clients' best interests. Laws vary widely between provinces and states.

Join a Professional Association

It's worthwhile to join professional organizations such as ARIDO (Association of Registered Interior Designers of Ontario), CDECA (Canadian Decorators' Association), ASID (American Society of Interior Designers), or CID (Certified Interior Decorators International) to take advantage of their guidance.

These recognized associations provide continuing education, bulk buying power, and a wealth of knowledge around bylaws, taxes and insurance. Many also provide referral services to potential clients.

One thing is certain, if you recommend a trade for some task – large or small – you are liable for that trade's performance, to some degree. Gulp. The lack of definition around "to some degree" makes me uncomfortable, and it ought to make you uncomfortable too. Because you are presenting yourself to clients as an expert and making a recommendation, there is a reasonable assumption that your recommendation will observe and perform to professional standards. If that's the case, in my opinion, then you should receive a premium (a fee) to incur that risk.

I must warn you, there are many who do not like this approach.

Professional organizations and insurance companies often dissuade design practices from project management, which increases liability. However, unless you refuse to recommend any trade and work only with the client's trades and insist on a contract that absolves you from any and every liability, you will be held responsible "to some degree" for the work performed. Even if you are simply "managing" or "providing some direction" to the client's trades, it is conceivable that you would be held liable in the event there is a problem.

Let me ask you this: would a client hire you to provide any project management if you accepted no responsibility for the work performed or its timing? Pretty unlikely. In my experience, it's not possible to perform the tasks required of a project manager without assuming *some* responsibility.

Fees for Project Management

Contractors and project managers (including design professionals who assume this role) hire subcontractors (also known as trades) to complete tasks on behalf of clients. In exchange for the management service the contractor or design professional acting as project manager charges a "markup". Markup typically refers to a percentage or fee over and above the cost of an item or service; which contributes income to the contractor or design professional acting as project manager. That "markup" figure likely includes calculations for *overhead* (fixed fees to run the company such as accounting fees, advertising, depreciation, insurance, rent, repairs, supplies, taxes, telephone bills, etc.) and *profit* (targeted percentage of earning for each job).

While there is no industry standard to determine what percentage markup should consist of, it's generally dictated by the size and complexity of a project. I've worked on projects where the markup is as little as 10% and as high as 40%.

> **Let's say an item or service costs $2,000 and the markup is 20%. In that case, the project manager's fee is $400.**

Most clients are very comfortable with this system as a general concept. They do not expect anyone to work for free. Since we agree (we do agree now, don't we?) that problems arise from miscommunication, it's critical the client understands what the actual percentage of markup is and how that percentage is going to be calculated and invoiced. **In other words hide nothing, disclose everything.**

If the design professional is acting as project manager, the same billing practices apply. In that case, we are charging for our billable hours plus an additional fee to manage the project and assume liability and responsibility for the project.

In a *transparent system*, the client has access to all original documentation and the fees are clearly and accurately outlined in the contract. When "markup" is explained as part of a professional contract, the client is able to quantify this cost and justify the expense.

In my office, our method for charging "markup" is based on our system of sharing discounts fifty-fifty.

Simply stated: We share any difference between the retail (gross cost incurred by clients working directly with the trade) and the wholesale (net cost provided to professional design firm). In other words, we share the discount or "savings" fifty-fifty.

Here's how we do this. We ask our trades to quote on jobs and give us a *better price* than they would if they dealt directly with a client who is not working with a design professional. We then calculate the difference between the standard client rate and the wholesale design firm rate and share that difference. Why would the trades be willing to work for us at a lower rate than they would charge a regular client? Oh, that's easy.

 Trades are willing to provide a professional design firm favourable pricing because we:

- Provide straightforward and easy to understand direction that is not open to interpretation.

- Manage all the billing and invoicing for the client.

- Collect all the fees and expenses.

- Keep the project moving forward since product is available when required and fees are up to date.

- Pay our trades at regular and quantifiable intervals.

- Manage and mediate any "issues" and take the difficult meetings with clients.

- Provide continuous, ongoing work.

- Obtain publicity around work provided.

These are just some of reasons busy trades like dealing with professional design firms.

Often, the trades are willing to come down 10% to 30% of the job cost in order to work directly for the design firm. This is particularly true in cases where you are providing that trade with repeat business. How can they do this?

Most trades build in allowances (up charges or higher fees) for clients who are not working with a design professional. Why? The experienced tradesperson knows there are going to be additional meetings to attend and more time spent, product which is not ordered in a timely fashion resulting in project delays, headaches around billing and collecting – the list goes on. In fact, trades often confide in me that they almost always spend more time and effort on projects where there is no design professional, shrinking the margin of profit anyway. Most are only too happy to develop a long-term relationship with a professional design firm.

Let's say, the trade is willing to provide your firm with a job and bill 10% less than he would if he were working directly for the client. In that case, your markup as the project manager totals 5%. On the other hand, if the trade is willing to work for 30% less, that markup fee jumps to 15%. In either scenario, **the client is still paying less than if the tradesperson worked directly for them without your involvement.**

> Can you see how the greater the tradesperson's discount is, the higher your profit and the better the client's savings? Let me give you an example.

Let's say the tradesperson has a job where the cost of the project is going to be $100,000 working directly for the client. You step into the picture, the professional design firm. You ask the tradesperson to "sharpen his pencil" in order to work directly with you and reap the benefits we reviewed earlier.

If the trade professional agrees he may say, "I can shave 10% from this job total and still be comfortable with my markup."

The tradesperson's adjusted price for the same job is:

$$\$100,000 - 10\% = \$90,000$$

The discount or savings generated by the new price is:

$$\$100,000 - \$90,000 = \$10,000$$

Since you are sharing the savings with the client 50/50, the client saves as follows:

$$\$10,000 \times 50\% = \$5,000$$

As the project manager your fee is $5,000 and the client saves the same amount.

> The client pays less than she would have working directly with the tradesperson ($95,000 instead of $100,000) and your company has some revenue to offset liability and contribute to profit at year's end.

Ah…. but there's a catch. When you step in as the project manager, you are responsible for the work performed. That's a sobering thought.

But keep in mind what I said earlier, if you even *recommend* a tradesperson for a job or give that tradesperson "direction" – unless you have a contract absolving you of all responsibility – then you are responsible anyway, at least in part.

The income you generate as the project manager is not enormous, but it does allow you some freedom in the event something unexpected occurs. It is not uncommon that you will need to use part of that "profit" during the execution of the job to keep things on track.

Let's stay with the example above and agree that you've acted as project manager on a job where the markup to you is 5% of $100,000 or $5,000.

Now, let's say that during the execution of the job your best painter suddenly throws his back out and can't finish the work. Uh oh, you've given the client a firm completion date. What to do?

You can go to the client and explain the situation and they may be completely comfortable waiting an indefinite period for the painter's back to heal. Or not. What if there is a pressing reason the work must be completed? A wedding in the back yard, the holidays fast approaching? In that case, as the project manager, you will want to secure another trade to complete the job. Only now, it's a last minute rush and everyone you know is busy working on other projects.

> In order to secure a good painter at the last minute, you may have to offer that trade an "incentive" or "premium" to get the work done on time and on budget, just as you've promised the client.

Let's say that "premium" is a straight $1,000 over and above what your own painter was going to charge for the outstanding portion of work. Thankfully, as you have a small percentage of income set aside from project management ($5,000) you have the funds to pay this extra fee, complete the job on time, on budget, exactly as promised with consistently pleasing results and keep the client happy.

On the other hand, if you are *not receiving a fee* for project management, and your painter throws his back out, what then? Well, you may go the client and explain the situation and ask for more money in order to meet the deadline. That might be an easy conversation or a difficult one. The client could happily write you an extra check, or could refuse to write an extra check because your agreement is to get the job done for a *specific fee*.

If you are like many design professionals, you will volunteer to pay this extra amount from your own pocket. Problem is, you won't really be happy with that scenario (despite telling me how much you love the job and it's not about money) and may begin to feel "taken advantage of" before long.

By charging a reasonable fee for project management you can:

a.   Avoid feeling anger and resentment on the job site - working more effectively on behalf of your clients.

b.   Comfortably solve problems that require additional money in the event somebody makes a mistake or something goes wrong – and still deliver on your promise to complete the job on time and on budget.

c.   Earn a reputation as a designer who is "no nonsense", who keeps her (his) word and completes the job without fuss.

In fact, in the earlier example where your painter is hurt, by stepping up and solving the problem without involving the client you may earn additional respect from your clients (and trades), which you would gladly pay a small sum for, yes?

If you are like most of the design professionals I've met while teaching **Kimberley Seldon Business of Design**™ courses you are pulling money out of your pocket on behalf of clients on a regular basis. The faucets you ordered came without an important bolt, so off you go to the hardware store to secure the needed item. Or, the crew's looking tired so you arrive on site with lunch and drinks. Or, someone breaks the client's lamp by mistake – so you rush out to find a replacement.

Charging a fee for project management is a reasonable thing to do. Provided you arm the client with full knowledge of your fees and the extent of your responsibility, it's a system that works well. If you do not charge a fee for this service, but accept responsibility, you are putting your firm (and employees) at risk by eating into the company's profit margins. It's that simple.

Review your working methods regularly

We meet regularly with our stable of professional tradespeople and review our method of working. I never leave these meetings without a better understanding of the challenges that face our trades and some insight into how we might improve our services for clients.

If a trade lets you down by doing a poor or incomplete job, it's YOUR responsibility to repair the damage. **This means you have tremendous liability.** At times, you must use the money generated in this category to keep the project running smoothly, on time and on budget exactly as promised. It's not professional to go back to the client and ask for more money for something that's already been agreed to. It might mean hiring someone else at a higher rate (and not billing the client the difference) to come in and keep the project running smoothly or repair something that went wrong.

I once had a contractor do a terrible job tiling a client's new en suite bathroom. Not only did I have to pay for new tile to be purchased, I had to pay a higher rate to have someone else redo the tile. In that case, I spent much more than the percentage I gained as project manager to get the job back on track.

As frustrating as it was to the client, my willingness to take ownership of the problem maintained our relationship and I went on to work for this lovely couple again.

How you handle mistakes speaks volumes about the character and integrity of you and your company.

Clients are reasonable people. They want you to succeed. By developing a transparent system of billing practices you increase your chances of satisfying the client and delivering the job on time, on budget, just like you promised.

When clients want to use their own trades

We have had varying degrees of success when clients want to use their own trades.

 In some cases, we have gained a new resource and gone on to work with that tradesperson many times. In other cases, it has created a regrettable division.

Let me give you a simple example.

One client insisted on using his own electrician during a renovation and decorating project. No problem, right? The rest of the trades on the job were ours. During an installation and in the client's presence, the electrician opened a box containing a long-awaited crystal chandelier, which had just arrived on site. When he lifted the chandelier from the box, he noticed two of its small crystal balls were detached, and announced, "This thing is busted."

Naturally, this upset the client who paid good money for the chandelier and waited several months for its arrival. My own decorative artist happened to be working nearby and saw the distress on the client's face. She intervened and said, "I am phoning Kimberley right now. She will deal with this."

When I arrived on site we discovered that nothing was broken. The pieces had simply come free of the wire that held them in place. It took about two minutes to resolve the issue and another 15 minutes to assure the client the sky wasn't falling. It only takes one weak link -- a tradesperson trying to score points or assert authority -- to spoil the whole job site. This is a very small example.

It's probably not that difficult for you to imagine (or perhaps you've encountered) a situation where the client's tradesperson made every problem your fault. Since you are not on site to defend yourself, the tradesperson is free to put forth a compelling argument against you. In other words, you will be thrown under the bus.

You may or may not hear of the incident. Either way, it's not a good scenario for you – or for the client. After all, is the client really getting the best value for their money when mistakes are happening on site and the source of the mistakes is obscured?

The tradesperson who throws you under the bus may have gotten away with something, but it's likely not the only problem that is going to occur. **Conversely, and I hope it goes without saying, if the error is yours, you must acknowledge it and take any pains to correct the damage.**

If you choose to work with the clients' trades

Make sure your contract clearly outlines your limited responsibility if you choose to work with the client's trades. For example, at **KSDG** we do not accept any responsibility for work performed by anyone not provided by us. Furthermore, we do not accept any responsibility for the timing of the work, or how their presence may impact the work or timing of our trades. We stand behind the work of our trades, but we do not stand behind the work of the client's trades. In the event a client's trade interferes with the progress of our trades, a financial penalty may result.

But what could go wrong?

Let's say you are working with the client's flooring specialist and that tradesperson has committed to finishing his portion of work by a particular date. Following the flooring work, you've hired a painter to come in and complete his work.

If the painter arrives and cannot work because the flooring specialist is running behind, that painter has set aside time in his busy schedule to accommodate your project and is not going to be happy about the delay. He is well within his right to ask for compensation based on losing a day's (or a week's) work.

> **Once you discuss the potential pitfalls with clients, they almost always opt to use your trades.** Wouldn't you pay a premium to have a single, reputable individual 100% responsible for the outcome of your project? Additionally, a cohesive team works together for the good of the whole project, saving the client time, money and trouble.

Section 6: Collections and Cash Flow

Earlier in **Chapter 4**, I mentioned that years ago my husband (putting in unpaid hours at my firm) informed me that I didn't have enough money to pay staff at the end of a pay period. I was speechless. I could not fathom how I was so low on funds to pay important bills when I was working so hard. That was one of the lowest moments I remember in business. I felt utterly foolish that I was so clueless about money.

Looking closely at my bank account versus my receivables, I was able to see that although we had sent invoices to customers, they remained unpaid – sometimes for months. So, I got on the phone to clients and I started to ask for the money. This was a humbling and illuminating experience.

Fortunately, I found the majority of clients were willing to pay their outstanding bills and to share with me their "experience" of my billing practices. I learned from multiple sources that my invoices never arrived with any regularity. A customer might receive one invoice for June billables in late July and then July's invoice a few days later. In addition, they were never clear about when those invoices were due or how many more invoices they might expect until the project was completed. **These inconsistencies and questions left my customers feeling out of control when it came to budgeting for the project.**

Since many of my customers are business people – lawyers, bankers, captains of industry – I asked for advice on how I might clear up these problems and improve the experience of working with my firm.

In exchange for this advice, I offered to comp one month's bill.

Here's what 9 Money Experts (aka Clients) taught be about invoicing:

- Invoice with regularity. Clients want to know when to expect invoices in order to manage their own Cash Flow.

- Be clear about when an invoice is due; clients need to know your expectations around due dates and occasionally, need a gentle reminder that an invoice is due.

- Manage money with integrity; clients love transparency and it builds trust.

- Produce clear and detailed invoices that are easy to understand.

In many cases, your clients are better off financially then you are. They do not expect you to "be a bank" and finance their projects, but they will let you do that if you choose to.

 Being a bank for one client might be manageable, but I don't advise it because it sets a dangerous precedent. And if you have multiple clients, then it's a proposition guaranteed to get you face time with your old friends Bitter, Angry, Disappointed and Resentful.

To avoid cash flow emergencies, collect deposits and ask for account balances at regular intervals.

Collect a deposit before ordering merchandise

Mature businesses collect a deposit *before* placing an order. Most firms ask for a deposit in the range of 50% to 75%.

 I can't tell you how many times I've worked with a designer who has ordered something for a client without receiving a deposit and then been furious because the customer changed her mind.

A deposit is a clear indication that the client is ready to order the item. To order anything without a deposit leaves you open to disappointment and potentially lost revenue.

In Summary:

1. Collect a Deposit
2. Place the Order

Once the order arrives, you will need to pay the balance.

In many cases, suppliers will ask you to pay the balance before they release the goods (that's so they don't have to be a bank for you!). If you don't have this money you are borrowing from your operating capital and creating potential **Cash Flow** problems. Compound that with a lag in payment from clients and you can see how you might have a major money crunch.

In our contract, we specify a date two-weeks before delivery or installation where we ask for the balance of an invoice. It's critical that you collect the balance from your client *before delivery or installation*.

In Summary:

1. Collect a Deposit

2. Place the Order

3. Collect Balance (two weeks prior to installation or delivery)

4. Deliver and/or Install

 I have not met one client who did not understand and appreciate our need for this policy.

If you provide a **turnkey service** (where furnishings are warehoused until all items can be delivered simultaneously) then your clients will be in the awkward position of having paid 100% for their furniture without having possession if it. I'll bet if you put yourself in the same position you could appreciate how it might be mildly uncomfortable.

It's imperative that you talk to your clients about this process at the project's initiation phase (as outlined in your contract) and then again as the date for collection approaches.

Acknowledge the trust they are placing in you. Remind them of the completion date and the process for completion as outlined in the contract. In my experience, clients are able to see this period through with relative ease because by this point in a project we have earned their trust repeatedly.

Remember, every difficulty with money stems from a lack of communication. Create a firm, non-flexible policy for invoicing and collecting.

Love Your Job, Love Your Life

It would have been easy for me to write a book of comedy, entertaining you with client stories from the ridiculous (yes, I've seen a couple naked) to the sublime (a trip to Paris!). Occasionally projects go terribly wrong and some clients seem impossible to manage. Still, I remember why I went into this business and you do too.

We want to create something beautiful and to make people happy through the creation of that ideal. The dream is still attainable. I'm suggesting that operating a business through a system of *Satisfaction by Luck* can never help you achieve your goals. But transforming your business practices through a system of **Satisfaction by Design** can and will allow you to build a thriving business *and* enjoy a more balanced life.

As a design professional, our career is not an easy one. But, it is a rewarding and exciting one. In **Kimberley Seldon's Business of Design™: Part 1** we explored the fundamentals of developing Mature Business Practices. Incorporating some or (even better) all of these practices will set you miles apart from the competition.

Finally, keep your perspective – and your sense of humour!

Early in my career clients asked me to get down on my hands and knees, peer through a magnifying glass and explain why the grout lines in their hand-laid marble floor were not "perfect." I explained that stone is a natural product with subtle differences apparent on each edge and face of a tile. I said that the process of laying stones by hand results in subtle variances along the grout line. That in fact, it's these subtle variances that give it a handcrafted appearance versus the machine precision of a factory floor. I could see my rationale was not working on them. Finally, I gently suggested that most of our clients enjoy their marble floor from a standing position without the aid of a magnifying glass. When the couple burst out laughing, I knew we were back on track.

On the next page is an article I wrote for **Style at Home** magazine, which received a lot of support from design professionals. Perhaps you will find it helpful as well.

THE DESIGNER CLIENT RELATIONSHIP

(Reprinted from Style at Home magazine)

By Kimberley Seldon

You've fallen in love with English country style. Or with flea market finds artfully displayed in a Paris apartment. But then there's that mod London flat that caught your eye... and the Thai teak bedstead that's so romantic. You've got a stack of design magazines by your bed – every month there's a new look you want to try. How can you realize your aspirations and maintain your sanity? You realize you need professional help, but that's complicated too, isn't it?

Decorating a home is a demanding, time-consuming, emotional and complicated process. Surrounding yourself with a professional team is the best way to ensure you'll wind up with the project you envision. To honour the client and designer relationship, here are some insights into "Designiquette."

It takes a team – don't go it alone

Recently, we were hired after a project was initiated and were dismayed that one of the large home's four bedrooms had no windows and its en suite could only be entered through a closet. While I'm not suggesting this is a typical experience, I do stress that a large renovation project should be initiated with a complete team that includes the designer, architect and contractor, and that each professional should come with a unique perspective and roles that are not interchangeable. A client benefits most when team members work harmoniously towards a common vision, so make sure to foster cohesiveness through ongoing team meetings and clear communication.

Be clear about your expectations

State objectives such as allotted budget, desired time line and a clear description of your likes and dislikes at the outset of the project. Determine a reasonable budget and share the information with your designer. If you have $10,000 to spend, say so. This way the designer can recommend appropriate strategies to maximize your spending power. It's best to avoid spreading a small budget over several rooms as one finished room is much more satisfying than three rooms which are only just started.

Charging for professional services

Designers are not paid for their time; they are paid for their expertise, which is quantified by increments of time; that is, we charge by the hour. A contract should spell out design fees in detail. Many firms charge a range of fees; one fee for the senior designer, another for junior designers and often a third fee for administration services.

In addition to upfront work -- onsite meetings, producing drawings, or selecting fabrics -- allow for "behind-the-scene" work. As an example: a client asked me about being billed 15 minutes to receive fabric for her sofa, determine it was the wrong fabric, phone the fabric company to arrange for the return of the wrong fabric and to acquire the correct fabric, phone the upholsterer to release his scheduled work, and notify her of the delay. When I asked: "Would it have been preferable for us to have sent the fabric directly to the upholsterer and allow him to cover the new sofa in the wrong fabric?" she understood perfectly. This brings me to my next point… trust.

Building trust – it's a two-way street

Like any relationship, this partnership requires trust. The client requires assurance that all project details are well in hand and the designer intends to fulfill on her promises. The designer requires the authority to manage the project including trades and suppliers as experience deems wise. Open communication is critical to everyone's comfort so speak up the moment you feel something is amiss. It's likely there is a simple explanation. On the other hand, if your concerns are not properly addressed, look for another designer.

Trust is also fostered by a thorough contract that spells out project details – from billing structure to trade policies, supplier guarantees to work ethics, design discounts to dispute resolutions. If you are not clear on any aspect of the contract, ask more questions and get clarification in writing.

The disagreement (aka designers are not marriage counselors)

She wants wood floors; he wants stone. Two pairs of eyes fixate on you, daring you to disagree. The successful completion of any design project calls for continued compromise. Try to cultivate collaboration at the outset by reaching some decisions in advance of the design-build process. One way for couples to reach agreement is to compare inspiration photos; images of rooms or ideas that each loves. Review the photos and determine common denominators – perhaps you both like dark wood, pale colours and colour photography. Couples who ease through a renovation project are flexible; they allow a fair number of "wins" for each person.

Interior design may look easy – it's not.

Ever waited in vain for the air conditioner repairman to arrive or had difficulty reaching a live customer service rep when your automated blinds got stuck in the down position? Then you understand the kinds of stress a design professional deals with daily. We often walk a tightrope between our clients' needs and the limitations of ordinary people (aka trades and suppliers).

The following steps for choosing a pillow illustrate my point:

STEP 1   Select fabric(s) – chenille, velvet, cotton, patterned, plain, red, blue?

STEP 2   Select trim(s) – self-pipe, rope, braid, bullion, tassel, rosette?

STEP 3   Determine size – 18" square, 24" x 18" rectangle, 16" bolster?

STEP 4   Choose filling – 100% down, polyester, poly cotton blend, density?

STEP 5   Choose edge detail - knife, box, Turkish, tasseled, beribboned?

STEP 6   Create purchase orders for fabrics, trims, forms and pillow maker

STEP 7   Order CFAs (cutting for approval) to ensure ordered fabric looks like the sample. 90% of the time, it's accurate, but about 10% of the time it's the wrong fabric or the wrong colour. Why? Because the fabric company had the wrong number written on the sample, or the firm discontinued the fabric, or someone simply entered the wrong number into a computer.

STEP 8   Receive fabrics, trims and forms; determine all are accurate.

STEP 9   Send all items and detailed instructions to pillow maker

STEP 10   Review finished pillows to ensure they are made to specifications.

STEP 11   Ship pillows to client's home.

STEP 12   Receive pillows on location and present to client for approval.

Multiply these organizational tasks exponentially for more complex items and you see what I mean.

State Your Intentions

We all take courses and attend lectures that leave us excited about a new direction and committed to change. Unfortunately, in most cases that adrenaline quickly dissipates when we re-enter the world. If you are truly committed to changing your business practices, to operating with transparency and producing a system of **Satisfaction by Design** than you must take action - now.

Fill in your intentions on the form provided below. Outline key actions to take immediately and give yourself a firm timeline for their completion. Once your form is complete, send it to a trusted peer or colleague and ask that person to hold you accountable, by checking your progress on the dates provided.

State your Intentions

1.   I intend to _____ by end of day tomorrow, _____.
              (take what action)   (date)

2.   I intend to _____ by end of one week, _____.
              (take what action)   (date)

3.   I intend to _____ by end of one month, _____.
              (take what action)   (date)

This form is available for download at www.businessofdesign.com/worksheets.

Thank you for you allowing me to be part of your support network. I'd love to celebrate your future accomplishments. Please visit www.businessofdesign.com to share your success stories.

I wish you continued success in business and in life.

Kimberley Seldon

Afterword

By Marysia Czarski, Velocity Partnership

The Coach's Perspective

Perhaps you are at a point in your career where you think you might benefit from the experience of working one-on-one with a professional Business Coach. Let me tell you how Kimberley's journey started.

I vividly remember the first time I spoke to Kimberley Seldon on the phone about the possibility of becoming her Business Coach. I know the referral from a mutual friend gave her a measure of confidence in my abilities. I was excited about the possibility of working with someone who had her media exposure. Watching her television show, **Design for Living** and seeing her live on **CityLine**, I knew I would be working with a witty, bright and energetic woman!

I don't think Kimberley really knew what she was getting herself into – and that's typical. The Coach – Client experience is non-linear; meaning it's not a series of straightforward steps that gets you to a specific result. Instead, it is customized to address both the immediate challenges in the business and the long-term opportunities for growth and betterment.

> Working with a professional Coach allows you to reach greater creative depths, by breaking bonds to "the daily grind". When that's accomplished your business becomes "life giving", rather than simply a means of meeting personal expenses. Doesn't that sound like value for your investment?

During the process we discover insights to personality and management styles -- things you are probably not aware of, yet they are blocking you from greater success. I call these blind spots. Blind spots can be exciting to discover, or completely unsettling since they unmask the root of a problem. Unearthing them allows you to abandon obsolete practices and take on new management behaviors; thus transforming your business (and your life).

When I work with new clients I insist on a 5-month contract (commitment). I still have Kimberley's initial contract – the one where she scribbled, "What if I'm not happy after 1-2 months?" in black pen. (I guarantee when Kimberley wrote that she didn't expect to see it in her own **Business of Design** book!) Clearly, we made it past the first five months.

I explained to Kimberley that working with a Coach is a bit like beginning an exercise plan. If you use a treadmill for 30 minutes a day for a couple of months, you'll start to notice a difference in how you feel. If you stop, you will lose all the benefits of those two months and pre-empt the real return that typically arrives after 4-5 months. Your mind and attitude, like your muscles, needs exercise to work optimally. I've learned that the more time I spend with clients, the more coachable they become, and the quicker they uncover insights that lead to transformation.

As a professional Coach, I can't just give you the 'Velocity Way', any more than I can work out for you. However, through a systematic approach to Coaching we can resolve immediate challenges, improve or transform long-standing issues and restore balance to your life. Although my coaching occurs from the context of business, I have yet to work with a client whose personal life isn't integrated into their business life. They really can't be separated. While I am not a therapist, I do seek to ensure personal issues aren't standing in the way of business success.

Here are the questions I asked Kimberley to answer before we started working together:

- Are you ready to seek out your blind spots and acknowledge gaps in learning?

- Can you take a step back from the "daily grind" and make time to grow your business?

- Are you ready to take 100% responsibility for the success and failure of your business?

- Can you accept that expertise at a trade does not make you a good manger of people?

- Are you willing to share intimately with your Coach – your hourly fees, management style, financial status, and so on -- in order to grow your business?

- Are you open to the possibility that your way may not be the better way?

- Do you want more from your business than just a bigger paycheck?

If you answered yes, like Kimberley did, hiring a Coach may be the right choice.

So how do you choose a Business Coach?
Referral is the best way to find a Business Coach that's right for you. If someone you know and trust makes a recommendation, it's likely a good fit. Failing that, ask business owners (not necessarily design professionals) whose acumen you admire if they've ever worked with a professional Coach. You might be surprised to learn that many people work with Coaches but don't share that information without prompting.

Before you hire, interview the prospective Coach's clients. Determine what results they would attribute to the working relationship and ask questions about the coaching style. Some coaches prefer to listen and allow the client to "discover" answers at their own pace. Others, like me, prefer a more integrated approach, providing correction, expert advice, assigning homework and lending guidance to support the decision making process.

Don't be discouraged if you find a Coach who doesn't live in your city. My Coach is based in Santa Cruz, California, and I'm in Toronto. I coach Canadian and American clients by phone. Kimberley and I conduct most of our meetings this way and our offices are only 20 minutes apart.

I consider it a privilege and an honor to work with my dynamic roster of clients and share in their achievements. Mostly, I love the sense of satisfaction that comes from seeing their lives improve -- along with their business.

Wishing you success in all you do,

Marysia Czarski

Velocity Training
www.velocity-partnership.com

Preview of Kimberley Seldon's Business of Design™: Part 2

Developing your "Unique Experience"

Chapters Include:

- Your Unique Experience – How you separate yourself from the Competition
- Systematic approach to Job Completion and Client Satisfaction
- Closing the Deal – Signing new clients and getting a "yes" from current clients
- Contracts – what must you include
- Retainers – how to Calculate, when to Collect, how to Use
- The Big Finish – succeeding expectations

And More!

Let's face it. Lots of people are "designers/decorators/stagers/stylists/organizers/landscapers/architects," making a living the same way you and I do. You may have great taste and style but so do many others. Over the years I've learned that *what* we do is not nearly as important as *how* we do it. If you want to stand out from the competition, you must provide clients with a "**Unique Experience.**"

In **Kimberley Seldon's Business of Design™: Part 2**, I share the details behind each phase of my own **15-Step Unique Experience**.

These 15-steps will provide you with a basis for building your own **Unique Experience**.

Kimberley Seldon
DESIGN GROUP

The KSDG Experience

Mission Statement:
At KSDG we strive to serve our valued and respected clientele through a system of **Satisfaction by Design.** We rely on experience, expertise and impeccable integrity to complete projects on time, on budget, with consistently pleasing results.

At KSDG, our goal is to make the design-build process an enjoyable one for our clients. Experience has shown us that knowledge of standard procedures helps clients feel comfortable for the duration of the project. Here's how we work:

STEP 1   Consultation with Kimberley Seldon or Senior Designer

STEP 2   Signing of agreement, receipt of retainer and commencement of project

STEP 3   On-site measurements, photos and final criterion meeting

STEP 4   Execution of floor plans and elevations, sourcing fabrics and furnishings

STEP 5   Presentation of estimates and furnishings/materials; collection of deposits

STEP 6   Placement of orders

STEP 7   Review of budget

STEP 8   Initiation of construction and renovation

STEP 9   Installation period continues and receipt of orders

STEP 10   Furniture installation and styling

STEP 11   Client reveal

STEP 12   Deficiencies walk through

STEP 13   Resolving deficiencies

STEP 14   Client closure meeting and presentation of final invoices

STEP 15   Presentation of Client Binder and thank you

Thank You!

I have been fortunate to find a voice in my chosen career. But, the lessons I share in these workbooks were initiated by others.

Thank you to **Marysia Czarski**, my business coach for her unwavering support and intelligent pushing. I am also deeply indebted to my friend **Beth Halstead** for pointing me gently (ok, not really gently) to Marysia.

Thank you to **Alex Newman** for her red pen and thoughtful massaging of this book. And to **Brian Koturbash** who took time away from baking award-winning apple pies (or building brands and businesses through exceptional creative and strategy) to provide me with invaluable feedback. And to brilliant editors who've inspired me to work on my craft: **Angela Lawrence, Julia Armstrong, Brett Walther** and the great, late **Rick Orchard**.

Cheryl Horne has been a constant source of wisdom and support while preparing the seminars and writing the workbooks. I am grateful to her and to my design team – Linda Jennings, Aysun Kuck, Erin Mercer, Kathy Seale, and Bret Tinson - for their kind and intelligent commitment. Heaps of praise to Tania LaCaria who did the book's comic illustrations.

Thank you to **clients and trades** who teach me more with each passing year. In particular, thank you to **Mike Tafts** from G. Pederson Construction Associates for reviewing references to trades and billing practices.

Thank you also to **Michael E. Gerber** (who I have yet to meet) for writing "The E Myth Revisited, Why Most Small Businesses Don't Work and What to Do About It". (Visit e-myth.com and michaelegerber.com to learn more about E-Myth).

Finally, as blessed as I have been in my career, I am infinitely more fortunate in life. Thank you to my children, **Cooper** and **Raleigh** for being patient with me when deadlines interfered with fun. And to my husband **Bob** (affectionately known as Captain Crisis around KSDG) who makes everything possible.

 Oops, one more thank you to my **Tassimo coffee maker**. While writing this book I consumed approximately 179 cappuccinos. I could never have finished this project without the energy you provided me.

18583689R10129

Made in the USA
San Bernardino, CA
22 January 2015